Occasional Paper Series   9

Gorbachev's International Outlook: Intellectual Origins and Political Consequences

Allen Lynch

WITHDRAWN

Institute for East-West Security Studies
New York   *1989*

This publication is made possible through the generous
support of the Ford Foundation and the John D. and Catherine T. MacArthur Foundation.

Distributed by Westview Press
    Frederick A. Praeger, Publisher
    5500 Central Avenue
    Boulder, Colorado 80301

Library of Congress Cataloging-in-Publication Data

Lynch, Allen, 1955–
    Gorbachev's international outlook.

    (Occasional paper series ; 9)
    1. Soviet Union—Foreign relations—1985–   .
2. Gorbachev, M. S. (Mikhail Sergeevich), 1931–   .
I. Title.   II. Series: Occasional paper series (Institute
for East–West Security Studies) ; 9.
DK289.L96   1989   327.47   89-7410

ISBN   (IEWSS) 0-913449-09-1
       (Westview) 0-8133-7795-1

Printed in the United States of America

TABLE OF CONTENTS

FOREWORD

For the first time since 1945 policy-makers and analysts in the West and East are confronted with fundamental choices about the nature of their relationship with the Soviet Union. It is increasingly accepted that Mikhail Gorbachev's "new political thinking" is not a passing phenomenon. The changes in Soviet foreign policy that come under the rubric of "new thinking" have a conceptual history that predates March 1985, when Gorbachev came to power. Soviet specialists succeeded in identifying this "ferment" under the surface of policy in the Brezhnev, Andropov and Chernenko years, and Allen Lynch, the author of this study, published a prize-winning monograph exploring that debate last year. Unfortunately, Western analysts still have not afforded sufficient attention to new Soviet definitions of the international system and its constituent elements. This deficiency results not only in Western analysis and policy underestimating the extent of change in the Soviet international outlook, but in the West continually being placed on the diplomatic defensive because of Soviet initiatives it has failed to foresee.

In this IEWSS Occasional Paper, Dr. Lynch builds on earlier research he has published in order to trace the links between "new thinking" and new policy. He explores what he calls the "intellectual origins" of "new political thinking," asks how the parameters of discussion among specialists and leaders have changed, and wonders how much support new thinking has within the Soviet leadership. After his comprehensive discussion of forces of change affecting Soviet foreign policy today, Dr. Lynch concludes with a discussion of the political consequences of the new thinking for the West.

Dr. Allen Lynch is Deputy Director of Studies at the Institute for East-West Security Studies and an Adjunct Professor in the Department of Politics at New York University. His book, *The Soviet Study of International Relations* (Cambridge University Press, 1987), won the Marshall D. Shulman Prize of the American Association for the Advancement of Slavic Studies for the most outstanding book on Soviet foreign policy published in 1987. He has also published a number of articles and two IEWSS Occasional Papers. He would especially like to thank Dr. F. Stephen Larrabee for his painstaking attention to the manuscript throughout. He also thanks Dr. Robert Legvold, Director of Columbia University's W. Averell Harriman Institute for Advanced Study of the Soviet Union; IEWSS Publications Officer Peter B. Kaufman; IEWSS Research Associate Ian Cuthbertson; IEWSS Program Officer Mary Albon; and the 1987–1988 and 1988–1989 Resident Fellows for helpful comments on earlier drafts of this paper.

The Institute gratefully acknowledges the support of the Ford Foundation and the John D. and Catherine T. MacArthur Foundation for the publication and distribution of this study. The Institute is pleased to sponsor the publication of this Occasional Paper as a contribution to the debate in both East and West about Soviet "new thinking"—clearly one of the most significant phenomena in the postwar period.

John Edwin Mroz
President
January 1989

... [O]ur foreign policy ... did not escape dogmatic and subjective attitudes. It trailed behind fundamental changes that occurred in the world and missed chances to reduce tensions and enhance understanding among nations. In our bid for military-strategic parity we occasionally failed to use opportunities available to attain security for our nation by political means, and, as a result, allowed ourselves to be lured into an arms race, which could not but affect this country's social and economic progress and its standing on the international scene.

—From "Theses of the CPSU Central Committee for the 19th All-Union Party Conference," *Pravda*, May 27, 1988.

1

Introduction

Mikhail Gorbachev has made it clear that, faced with a profound crisis of performance of the Soviet system, he seriously intends to carry out a thorough "restructuring" of Soviet society in an effort to make the Soviet economy capable of effectively exploiting the opportunities offered by contemporary science, technology, and management technique. Gorbachev has repeatedly underscored the need for structural economic reform and, just as important, for sweeping social and even political reforms in order to sustain the economy over the long run. When it comes to Soviet foreign policy under Gorbachev, however, the picture has not always been so clear. Some Western analysts have dismissed the "new political thinking" that Gorbachev has offered as the contemporary Soviet vision of world politics, contending that Soviet foreign policy during the past three years has simply been the continuation of age-old objectives under new names.[1] Thus, the *volte-face* adoption by Gorbachev of the NATO position on the INF issue was widely interpreted as just the latest Soviet effort to "split" the alliance. Similarly, the consistent Soviet devaluation of nuclear weapons as a durable guarantor of peace, including the admission by Gorbachev himself that parity may no longer—under conditions of an unregulated arms competition—assure strategic stability, has been taken mainly as an attempt to delegitimize the *West's* nuclear deterrent and provide the USSR with a psychological, and thus geopolitical, advantage in the East-West competition.

Surely, prudence in judgment is always justified in the evaluation of Soviet foreign policy. At the same time, there is also a danger in underestimating the extent of change in Soviet attitudes on international policy, as illustrated by the American debacle in responding to Soviet initiatives at the Reykjavik summit and the early self-inflicted allied paralysis in the face of Gorbachev's decisive shift in his INF position. If the United States and its allies are not to find themselves constantly on the diplomatic defensive, reacting to a policy agenda increasingly defined by the Soviet leadership, they will have to start paying careful attention to the conceptual ferment affecting contemporary Soviet foreign policy. A number of remarkable statements and actions—ranging from acceptance of the U.S. "zero option" on the INF issue, acceptance in several arms control fora of intrusive on-site challenge inspection, to delinking the Soviet military presence in Afghanistan from the character of the Kabul government, support for the United Nations and its peacekeeping activities, as well as the decision in December

---

1. Jean Quatras, "New Soviet Thinking Is Not Good News," *The Washington Quarterly* 11, No. 3 (Summer 1988), pp. 171–183. Quatras is the pseudonym of a "French specialist," evidently a government official. Also, Terry McNeil, "Gorbachev's First Three Years in Power: Not So New Political Thinking in Foreign Policy," *Radio Liberty Research*, RL76/88, March 2, 1988; and U.S. Department of Defense, *Soviet Military Power* (Washington, DC: U.S. Government Printing Office, 1987), p. 11: "In foreign policy, the new [Soviet] leadership has retained long-term Soviet objectives and strategies, although it appears to be acting with effectiveness. The Party leadership remains committed to the long-term objective of establishing the USSR as the dominant world power." See also the speech delivered by Robert M. Gates, Deputy Director of the CIA, on October 14, 1988, to the American Association for the Advancement of Science, "Recent Developments in the Soviet Union and Implications for U.S. Security Policy."

1988 to reduce the Soviet armed forces unilaterally by 500,000 troops (together with associated equipment)—suggest the scope of change in Soviet foreign-policy attitudes under Gorbachev.

This "new political thinking" may be seen as a determined effort by the Gorbachev leadership to redefine conceptually, as well as through a process of political interaction, the nature of the international environment facing the USSR and the range of appropriate Soviet choices in foreign and security policy. This new definition of the international system reflects both a revised evaluation of long-term international political and military trends, which has its roots in the pre-Gorbachev era, and the pressing character of Soviet domestic needs, as Gorbachev searches for ways of limiting the scope of demands placed upon the Soviet system as it proceeds on the path of structural reform—economic and political—at home. At the same time, the "new thinking" is intended to help provide Soviet foreign policy with a more appropriate set of ends and means.

Gorbachev has forged the "new political thinking" by drawing upon the pioneering conceptual work done during the Brezhnev and Andropov periods and adapting it to the basic foreign-policy priorities as determined by the Soviet political leadership. It is important to keep in mind that the "new political thinking" itself is first of all a political rather than an intellectual or conceptual act. It reflects preestablished political priorities of the Gorbachev leadership, which in turn has assiduously coopted strains of thinking—some of it actually new, much of it developed quietly by specialists during the Brezhnev period—which suit its purposes and long-term goals. Partly, this is aimed at making more persuasive, to both foreign and domestic audiences, the new course that Gorbachev has set for himself in foreign affairs. Encouragement of debate is also intended to provoke discussion in normally reticent quarters, such as the military, and thus to raise issues and elicit information that the political leadership requires in making effective national decisions. Furthermore, it is now clear that Gorbachev and his closest colleagues find the world view offered by the new thinkers in many respects a more persuasive interpretation of reality than that bequeathed them by their predecessors, as the epigraph to this paper suggests. But most of all, the "new political thinking" represents a determined political effort by the Soviet leadership to recast the nature of the threat environ-

3

ment said to be facing (and actually facing) the USSR and thereby monopolize domestic Soviet discussion of the future military, economic and political agendas of the Soviet state.[2]

The following analysis will show that there is a clear link between the revision of fundamental Soviet foreign-policy concepts that took place on the specialist level throughout the Brezhnev period and much of the "new" thinking on international relations expounded by Gorbachev and his associates. Such "new" ideas as the rejection of nuclear war as a conceivable act of policy, the heightened significance attached to political factors in security policy, and increasing recognition of the multipolar and interdependent character of contemporary international relations, all find lucid expression by currently influential Soviet policy analysts in the pre-Gorbachev era. Indeed, the emerging Soviet world view represents a synthesis of tendencies present in Soviet policy circles since the Twentieth Party Congress in 1956. Clearly, it has been changes in the international system as well as within the Soviet system that have triggered revisions in the formulation of Soviet foreign policy, first on the conceptual level and now in the actual making of policy itself. Since the source for many of these revisions arises from the USSR's external environment, i.e., from factors beyond Soviet control, they cannot be interpreted as simple "tactical" adjustments, ready to be reversed at an expedient moment.[3] Instead, they are part and parcel of an

---

2. For a similar viewpoint see Stephen M. Meyer, "The Sources and Prospects of Gorbachev's New Political Thinking on Security," *International Security* 13, No. 2 (Fall 1988), pp. 125, 128, 134, 137, 156.
3. Fyodor Burlatsky, one-time speechwriter for Khrushchev and now a leading figure in Gorbachev's *glasnost'* campaign, has argued that the influence of "external" factors on socioeconomic systems, including communist systems, "is greater than ever before." Similarly, Georgi Shakhnazarov, former deputy chief of the Central Committee department responsible for liaison with ruling communist parties, and now a Gorbachev advisor, clearly implies that, given the increasing impact of scientific-technical innovations in the military and economic fields on domestic social structures, states must increasingly adjust to the universal demands of the scientific-social revolution. Fyodor Burlatsky and A. Galkin, *Sotsiologiya. Politika. Mezhdunarodnye otnosheniya* [Sociology. Politics. International Relations.] (Moscow: Mezhdunarodnye Otnosheniya, 1974), pp. 235, 237–238; Georgi Shakhnazarov, "Politika skvoz' prizmu nauki" [Politics through the Prism of Science], *Kommunist*, No. 17 (1976), pp. 111–112. Specialists now speak of the "reverse influence" of the system of international relations on, e.g., Soviet-American relations. See P. T. Podlesnyi, "Vvedeniye" [Introduction], in G. A. Trofimenko and

ongoing process of adjustment, between both East and West, and thus should be of particular concern to Western analysts and officials at an exceptionally fluid moment in Soviet relations with the outside world.

As part of the analysis of the intellectual origins and political consequences of the "new political thinking," I shall consider the factors—external and internal—that helped lead to the emergence of this strain of thinking in the USSR. I shall then attempt to trace the connections between the "new thinking" and the policy level, and in the process address three questions:

- How have the parameters of discussion among Soviet foreign policy analysts and the leadership changed?

- What is the extent of support within the Soviet leadership for "new thinking," as reflected in published statements on Soviet foreign policy?

- To what extent has the new thinking affected the role that Soviet foreign-policy specialists play in policy-making?

P. T. Podlesnyi, *Sovetsko-amerikanskiye otnosheniya v sovremennom mire* [Soviet-American Relations in the Contemporary World] (Moscow: Nauka, 1987), p. 5.

2

Intellectual Origins of the "New Political Thinking"

■ *Lenin and Stalin*

The Soviet view of international relations has traditionally rested on Lenin's theory of imperialism.[4] Lenin put forward a view of international relations in which—in admittedly simplified form—the international behavior of states is primarily explained through the projection of the alleged internal contradictions of capitalism onto a crisis-prone, world capitalist system. In essence, it is the driving internal dynamic of capitalism, requiring foreign markets for surplus production, which in this view determines the issue of war and peace. Class relations are key; national interests are definitely subordinate. There is no qualitative distinction in this view between internal and international politics. International relations are essentially the product of the various socioeconomic systems organized as separate states. Consequently, one cannot speak of international relations as an independent field of analysis. It is, rather, a subordinate branch of political economy.[5]

"The analysis contained in Lenin's *Imperialism*," Paul

---

4. As developed in his *Imperialism: The Highest Stage of Capitalism*, contained in V. I. Lenin, *Imperialism and Imperialist War (1914–1917). Selected Works*, Vol. 5 (New York: International Publishers, no date).
5. Until 1988 the Soviet research institutes on international relations were subsumed under the economics division of the Academy of Sciences; on March 17, 1988, the decision was taken to establish a separate division for "World Economy and International Relations." See "V orbite Sovetskoi nauki" [In the Orbit of Soviet Science], *Pravda*, March 18, 1988, p. 3. See Part 6 of this paper for a discussion. For a more extensive treatment of what follows, see the author's *The Soviet Study of International Relations* (Cambridge: Cambridge University Press, 1987).

Marantz has written, "remained official dogma throughout Stalin's life."[6] Yet whereas Lenin's basic international outlook was self-confident, optimistic, opportunistic and flexible, Stalin's was defined by insecurity, pessimism, determinism and rigidity: it was the conviction of the lack of choices open to the Soviet state in an unremittingly hostile international environment that informed Stalin's world view and led to a stark, class-based doctrine of international relations. The main elements of this vision of world politics, according to Marantz, included:

1. The foreign policies of the Western states are economically determined by the capitalist system and aimed at eradicating socialism (i.e., the USSR) by any means, including war.
2. War between capitalist states, which would necessarily assume global proportions and thus engulf the USSR too, is inevitable due to the inner logic of imperialism.
3. Due to the perceived nature of the "capitalist" states, Soviet disarmament proposals can only have a propaganda function.
4. As a corollary of a thesis put forward regarding domestic politics, a high degree of tension is seen as inevitable given the mortal struggle between capitalism and socialism.
5. The conviction that war is the handmaiden of revolution.
6. Consequently, a failure to develop any doctrine of peaceful coexistence. In Stalin's words: "In order to eliminate the inevitability of wars, imperialism must be destroyed."[7]

It is hardly surprising, as even some Soviet analysts are beginning to admit,[8] that under these circumstances the international system would be characterized by an acute degree of

---

6. Paul Marantz, *From Lenin to Gorbachev: Changing Soviet Perspectives on East-West Relations* (Ontario: Canadian Institute for International Peace and Security, Occasional Paper No. 4, May 1988), p. 21.
7. Paraphrased from Marantz's excellent discussion in Marantz, *From Lenin to Gorbachev*, pp. 21–30.
8. Vladlen Sirotkin, "Puti mirovoi revolyutsii" [Paths of the World Revolution], *Izvestiya*, September 3, 1988, p. 3; Interview with V. I. Dashichev, a senior officer of the influential Institute on the Economy of the World Socialist System, in *Komsomolskaya Pravda*, June 19, 1988, p. 3, translated in Foreign Broadcast Information Service (FBIS), *Daily Report-Soviet Union*, June 29, 1988, pp. 56–58; V. Israelyan, a senior Soviet diplomat, "Mir ne mozhet byt' zaklyuchen tol'ko sverku" [Peace Cannot Only be Made From Above], *Literaturnaya Gazeta*, June 15, 1988, p. 14; and V. I. Dashichev in *Literaturnaya Gazeta*, May 18, 1988, p. 4, translated in *FBIS-SU*, May 20, 1988, pp. 4–8.

tension when Stalin's Soviet Union came to be, after 1945, one of two foundations of world politics.

A whole series of substantive conclusions follows from such a model of world politics. Among the most important is the proposition that the existence of (doomed) "capitalist" states throughout the world assures the inevitability of world war. Conversely, war between "socialist" states, which have abolished the anarchy of the market and thereby the mainspring of modern warfare, is a manifest impossibility. Yet surely the survival and even prosperity of the advanced capitalist states; the advent of the atomic and then hydrogen bombs; the eventual emergence of a hostile (communist) Chinese state along the Soviet border; and the resistance of most of the Third World to the Soviet model—all must have shaken certain assumptions of this Leninist/Stalinist model for Soviet leaders and analysts of world affairs.

■ *The Khrushchev Period*

Most observers, both Soviet and Western, see the year 1956, the year of the Twentieth Soviet Party Congress and Khrushchev's secret speech denouncing Stalin's crimes against the Communist Party, as the critical turning point in Soviet thinking on international relations.[9] Two ideological revisions—concerning the breaking of the "capitalist encirclement" by the Soviet Union and the non-inevitability of general war—were of special significance. They openly suggested, as had been implicit in Stalin's policy of socialism-in-one-country, that henceforth the revolutionary transformation of the world would be effected through international relations, rather than through the class struggle as such.[10] States had now become the formally recognized protagonists in the class conflict. The increased importance that relations among nation-states were held to have for the future of socialism required going beyond the "rather mechanistic (Leninist) transplant of theses regarding internal relations and laws of society to

---

9. William Zimmerman, *Soviet Perspectives on International Relations, 1956–1967* (Princeton: Princeton University Press, 1971), p. 275 and *passim;* Dimitri Tomashevski, *On the Peaceful Coexistence of States* (Moscow: Novosti, 1973), p. 34.
10. V. Kubalkova and A. Cruikshank, *Marxism-Leninism and the Theory of International Relations* (London: Routledge and Kegan Paul, 1980), p. 107.

external, intersocietal relations."[11] From this date also ensues the proliferation of Soviet research institutes devoted to the systematic study of international relations, a consequence of the transformation of international relations into a legitimate area of inquiry below the apex of the Party-government apparatus.[12]

The key trends emerging from this post-Stalin analysis of international relations included: *first*, the view of international relations as an arena populated by a plurality of corporate actors, with states (as opposed to the two camps) as dominant; *second*, increasing attention paid to the role of institutions as sources of foreign-policy conduct; *third*, recognition of the non-inevitability of world war in the nuclear age, which tends to undermine the Soviet view of international relations as a closed system, i.e., comprehensible by a general theory which posits a predictable solution at every point. Too many critical elements are in the hands of others; the idea of general war as the handmaiden of revolution is thereby negated. *Finally*, there appeared to be a marked tendency for Soviet perspectives on international relations to converge with much American analysis on (a) the course of international relations as indeterminate; (b) the basic (state) structure of the modern international system; (c) recognition of the role of internal politics in American foreign policy; and (d) preoccupation with the political significance of technology (especially weapons technology) and the constraints thereby imposed on the behavior of states in the atomic age.[13]

■ *The Brezhnev Era*

Soviet studies of international relations in the Brezhnev period continued to move away from the rigid determinism of orthodox Soviet political economy, the predominant pattern before 1956, toward conceptions that accord a greater importance to such categories as politics, the state, and the "system" of international relations. The organization of a symposium on the theory of international relations by the

11. Silviu Brucan, *The Dissolution of Power: A Sociology of International Relations and Politics* (New York: Alfred A. Knopf, 1971), pp. 48–49.
12. Oded Eran, *The "Mezhdunarodniki": An Assessment of Professional Expertise in the Making of Soviet Foreign Policy* (Tel Aviv: Turtle Dove Press, 1979); Zimmerman, *Soviet Perspectives*, p. 275.
13. Zimmerman, *Soviet Perspectives*, pp. 275–279, 282.

Institute of World Economy and International Relations in 1969 represented a turning point in the evolution of Soviet studies on the subject. International relations as a distinct field of scholarly inquiry began to be discussed for the first time. Theorists such as Georgi Shakhnazarov, long-time deputy head of the Central Committee Department responsible for liaison with ruling communist parties and now a top Gorbachev advisor, and the late Nikolay Inozemtsev, former head of the prestigious Institute of World Economy and International Relations, made major contributions in this regard.

The explicitness with which these analysts, as well as others, rejected traditional Soviet ideas about international relations is striking. Such ideas as the identification of international relations with inter*state* relations; the primacy of the national (as opposed to the class) factor as long as a world structured along the state principle exists; the transformation of international relations into an independent force, exercising a potentially decisive influence on the internal structures and prospects of states and socioeconomic systems; and the primacy of the political sphere over economic and class forces in the conduct of foreign policy—all of these ideas have found their way into the works of respected Soviet students of international relations and now into the foreign-policy analysis of Gorbachev himself.[14] Shakhnazarov has argued that, while a general class analysis of world politics retains its validity, the center of analysis in international relations must be *"political forces of an international character and the basic trends of their interaction."*[15] Indeed, Shakhnazarov has gone so far as to write that "patriotism will remain the major principle of Communist doctrine . . . as long as national statehood remains a political form of social development."[16] The thesis that, for Soviet Marxists, the international system is divided not according to criteria of power but rather according to levels of economic development, and that therefore the state is not the critical unit

---

14. "Problemy teorii mezhdunarodnykh otnosheniy" [Problems of the Theory of International Relations], *Mirovaya Ekonomika i Mezhdunarodnye Otnosheniya*, Nos. 9 and 11 (September and November 1969), pp. 88–106, 78–98, respectively.
15. Georgi Shakhnazarov, "Effective Factors of International Relations," *International Affairs* (Moscow), No. 2 (February 1977), p. 79 (emphasis added).
16. Ibid., p. 86.

of analysis, is seriously challenged by these authors' analyses. Nevertheless, the Marxist disdain for the prevailing international order has not been surrendered. Greater "realism" need not imply convergence on the normative level. In fact, the argument that Soviet theorists have employed in support of their innovations, as well as their borrowings from Western scholars, have been instrumentalist, i.e., that fresh approaches would improve the functioning of Soviet foreign policy.[17]

The Nature of the International System: The De-ideologization of Vision

Soviet international analysis during the Brezhnev era went considerably beyond the "two-camp" concept in identifying the basic structural elements of the international system. First, international relations are understood as containing a plurality of corporate actors, with states, as opposed to the two camps of "capitalism" and "socialism," as dominant. Second, the character of relations between and within "camps" of states has changed significantly. Though the United States and the Soviet Union occupy the central position on the world stage, each is challenged by forces emanating from other states and from the international system as a whole. As one analyst recently put it, "It is therefore necessary to see the objective limits of the influence of the USSR and the USA on the development of the international situation, and to take into account both traditional and new factors of world politics."[18] These forces, often issuing from states of the same socioeconomic order (or alliance), result in a relative weakening of the position of both the United States and the Soviet Union within their own alliance systems. The economic recovery of Western Europe and Japan after World War II, together with the loosening of tensions between the Soviet and American blocs, has led to an assertion of national

---

17. Vladimir Petrovsky, now Deputy Foreign Minister, has made the same point in his *Amerikanskaya vneshne-politicheskaya mysl'* [U.S. Foreign Policy Thinking] (Moscow: Mezhdunarodnye Otnosheniya, 1976), pp. 110–117.
18. Podlesnyi, "Vvedeniye," in Trofimenko and Podlesnyi, *Sovetsko-amerikanskiye otnosheniya*, p. 5.

claims against American interests on the part of its allies. The rise of nationalism in the former colonial countries, the increased military power of the Soviet Union, and internal constraints of public opinion in the West have served to hinder the ability of the United States to make its writ felt throughout the underdeveloped world.

Also, "difficulties" within the Soviet alliance system, traceable to the persistence of national interests and uneven levels of economic development, have diminished the coherence of the Soviet bloc and have even thrown into question some of the "achievements of socialism." This was brought out with particular clarity in the case of the Soviet-led invasion of Czechoslovakia in 1968. The "Brezhnev Doctrine," which asserted that "the entire [socialist] system was responsible for the maintenance of socialism in particular countries," in effect acknowledged a structural deficiency in the socialist state system, which required armed Soviet intervention to ensure its survival. This meant an enhanced appreciation of the indeterminacy of the competition between socialism and capitalism and the concession that now socialism, like capitalism, relied on "subjective" political (as opposed to "objective" socio-economic) forces for its survival. In this sense the Brezhnev Doctrine depicted the socialist world as a mirror image of "imperialism"—with "struggle" as the dominant motif—with the added proviso that the center of struggle could now be located within the socialist camp.[19] Similarly, the eruption of the Polish crisis in 1980–1981 sent shudders throughout the Soviet leadership, as it witnessed the progressive disintegration of the authority of the Polish Communist Party in the face of the mass workers' movement represented by Solidarity. The message was clear for all to see: as Konstantin Chernenko himself observed, the Polish crisis presented a negative-object

19. R. Judson Mitchell, *Ideology of a Superpower: Contemporary Soviet Doctrine on International Relations* (Stanford: Hoover Institution Press, 1982), pp. 31, 33–34. See also W. (V) I. Gantman, late head of section on international theory at the key Institute on World Economy and International Relations, "Typen Internationaler Konflikte," in Daniel Frei, ed., *Theorien der internationalen Beziehungen* (Munich: R. Piper and Co., Verlag, 1973), pp. 87, 90–91; N.I. Lebedev, N. P. Drameva, V. B. Knyazhinskiy, eds., *Mezhdunarodnye otnosheniya i bor'ba idey* [International Relations and the Struggle of Ideas] (Moscow: Izdatel'stvo Politicheskoy Literatury, 1981), p. 235, for an indication of a Soviet sense of weakness in the international ideological sphere.

lesson of what happens when a communist party loses contact with the masses. Even the Soviet Union might no longer be able to avoid such instabilities, which would strike at the heart of the power and cohesion of the alliance of Soviet-style party-states.[20]

The supplanting of classes by states as the chief actors in world politics has consequently been accompanied by a serious erosion in the ability of the two most powerful states to maintain the cohesion of their alliances. The challenge to the American position, however, does not necessarily strengthen the Soviet one. Indeed, to the degree that the same processes are at work on both countries, the international standing of the Soviet Union may be considerably weaker. As Yevgeny Primakov—director of the prestigious Institute of World Economy and International Relations and a close advisor to Gorbachev—wrote in the early 1970s, increased multipolarity in the international system enhances the significance of the "uncontrollable" factor in world politics, especially in crisis situations.[21]

What is most important in this emerging Soviet view, which holds despite the apparent resurgence of U.S. power in the Reagan years, is that American power is diminished by all of the salient processes in contemporary international politics. Nationalism, the economic recovery of Europe and Japan, the recovery of the Soviet Union itself and its vastly increased military potential—all permit a Soviet analyst to observe a qualitative transformation in the international position of the United States, which is to say an important change in the international system itself. Aleksandr Yakovlev, member of the Politburo, Chairman of the new Central Committee Commission on International Relations, and one of Gorbachev's most trusted associates, has spoken of the "relative decline" of the

---

20. For an example of high-level Soviet concern over the place of Poland in the Soviet alliance system, see Diplomaticheskaya Akademiya M.I.D. SSSR, *Vneshnyaya politika i diplomatiya sotsialisticheskikh stran* [Foreign Policy and the Diplomacy of the Socialist Countries] (Moscow: Mezhdunarodnye Otnosheniya, 1981), p. 93. See also Elizabeth Teague, "Perestroika: The Polish Influence," *Survey* 30, No. 3 (October 1988), pp. 39–58.
21. Vitaly Zhurkin and Yevgeny Primakov, *Mezhdunarodnye konflikty* [International Conflicts] (Moscow: Mezhdunarodnye Otnosheniya, 1972), p. 15. Zhurkin is the director of the new Institute of Europe, which began operations in 1988. Primakov, Director of IMEMO, is head of the new Academy of Sciences division for "World Economy and International Relations."

United States in world affairs, which he regards as a "normal development."[22] Whereas once, in the 1950s and early 1960s, the United States, employing a diplomacy predicated on the swift and credible deployment of armed force, could be said to occupy a "hegemonic" position, this is no longer so. One Soviet historian cites the "widespread recognition" among American scholars that American "hegemony" in Western Europe, as in international relations as a whole, is a thing of the past. Its defeat in Vietnam served to catalyze a number of latent tendencies in the international system which tend to constrain the application of American power.[23] In its search for an end to the Vietnam debacle, the United States approached the Soviet Union and began a process that culminated in American recognition of Soviet strategic nuclear parity. The concomitant political detente signified to America's allies that relations with the Soviet bloc could be cultivated without incurring American displeasure, while their economic recovery gave them the means to move in that direction. Specifically national interests could be furthered, thus reinforcing the loosening of "imperialist" alliances which to a certain extent had been both cause and consequence of detente.

The irony for the Soviets, and it seems to be well appreciated, is that in attempting to redress the balance of power in the wake of Vietnam, the United States took measures, specifically the opening to China, which had the effect of creating further and quite serious obstacles to the achievement of Soviet goals. "The very departure of such a country as the People's Republic of China," two Soviet theorists declared, "from the forces of peace to positions relying on the forces of war has damaged the international correlation of forces on issues of

---

22. Interview with Aleksandr Yakovlev, *La Repubblica* (Rome), May 21, 1985, p. 7, in FBIS, *Daily Report-Soviet Union*, May 24, 1986, pp. CC1–CC2.
23. S. I. Appatov, *S.Sh.A. i Yevropa: obshchiye problemy amerikanskoy kontinental'noy politiki* [The USA and Europe: General Problems of American Foreign Policy on the Continent] (Moscow: Mysl', 1979), p. 202. Along these lines, one political-military analyst, with ties to the General Staff, argued recently that there is a secular tendency, when compared to the 1950s, for a progressively diminishing U.S. reliance on "political-military actions" in support of its foreign policy, "in spite of the subjective efforts of the most aggressive circles of imperialism to increase the role of military force in their country's foreign policy objectives." I. Mochalov and A. Podberyozkin, "V. I. Vernadsky: antimilitarizm XX veka" [V.I. Vernadsky and Twentieth-Century Anti-Militarism], *Politicheskoye Samoobrazovaniye* (forthcoming issue).

war and peace."[24] Furthermore, the loosening of "imperialist" alliances took place within definite limits, so that antagonisms between the United States and its chief allies respected the fundamental distinction between what remained of the capitalist and socialist camps. From this point of view, the United States, though no longer a hegemon, still occupied a powerful, if not quite commanding position in world politics. This was so not because the United States can determine or influence the outcome of every conflict or dispute of importance to it, but rather because, as Kenneth Waltz has noted, the United States remains the only power which by itself can substantially alter the "rules" by which other states "play the game."[25]

Whence, in the Soviet view, does this special position of the United States derive? It is to be found in the fact that the United States, uniquely, stands astride the two critical axes of world politics: the strategic-military axis, composed of the United States, the Soviet Union and China; and the political-economic axis, composed of the United States, Western Europe and Japan.[26] In this economic-military-political constellation, the United States disposes of formidable leverage: first, in its own right, as a great power with great mobility of power; second, as the leader of a great alliance system which incidentally incorporates the two most powerful agglomerations of economic power in the world, after the United States and the Soviet Union; and third, as the privileged beneficiary of Sino-Soviet tension and the improvement of relations between itself and the People's Republic of China. Furthermore, the

24. N. M. Nikol'skiy and A. V. Grishin, *Nauchno-tekhnicheskiy progress i mezhdunarodnye otnosheniya* [Scientific-technical Progress and International Relations] (Moscow: Mezhdunarodnye Otnosheniya, 1978), p. 55. See also Andrey A. Kokoshin (now deputy director of the Institute of U.S. and Canada Studies), *S.Sh.A.: za fasadom global'noy politiki* [The USA: Behind the Facade of Global Policy] (Moscow: Izdatel'stvo Politicheskoy Literatury, 1981), pp. 24–25.
25. Kenneth Waltz, *Theory of International Politics* (Reading, Mass.: Addison-Wesley, 1979).
26. D. M. Proyektor, (a retired colonel in the Soviet armed forces, now at the IMEMO think tank), *Puty Yevropy* [European Paths] (Moscow: Znaniye, 1978), pp. 126–127; N. I. Doronina, *Mezhunarodnyy konflikt. O burzhuaznykh teoriyakh konflikta. Kriticheskiy analiz metodologii issledovaniy* [International Conflict. On Bourgeois Theories of Conflict. A Critical Analysis of Methodologies of Research] (Moscow: Mezhdunarodnye Otnosheniya, 1981), p. 10; I. G. Usachev, *Mezhdunarodnaya razryadka i S.Sh.A.* [International Detente and the USA] (Moscow: Mysl', 1980), pp. 138, 150, 167.

United States and its allies stand to profit more than the Soviet bloc from the application of the fruits of the increasingly important scientific-technological revolution.[27]

True, the course of "the national-liberation struggle" in the underdeveloped countries registered some marked successes for "progressive" and even pro-Soviet forces in recent years (e.g., Vietnam, Angola, Ethiopia). Yet the very strength of the "imperialist" economy worldwide provides the capitalist alliance system with "a powerful economic potential" in its policies toward the underdeveloped countries. On the whole, victories for "progressive" forces in the Third World have tended against imperialism rather than directly in favor of the socialist bloc.[28] Indeed, for Soviet policy intellectuals there is a real question as to the continued validity of the Soviet model for the developing countries.[29] At best, those developing countries that have started on the road of "non-capitalist development" only find the prospects for socialism opening up before them, and they represent a minority still.[30] In short, "imperialism's" ability to influence events in the developing world, though certainly not what it once was, remains quite considerable.[31]

The picture of the world that is presented in much Brezhnev-era analysis is quite far removed from that offered by the

27. Proyektor, *Puty Yevropy*, pp. 128, 159; V. I. Antyukhina-Moskovchenko, A. A. Zlobin, and M. A. Khrustalev, *Osnovy teorii mezhdunarodnykh otnosheniy. Uchebnoye posobiye* [Foundations of the Theory of International Relations. A Teaching Aid] (Moscow: Moskovskiy Gosudarstvennyy Institut Mezhdunarodnykh Otnosheniy, 1980), p. 79.
28. N. N. Inozemtsev *et al.*, eds., *Leninskaya teoriya imperializma* [The Leninist Theory of Imperialism] (Moscow: Mysl', 1977), p. 212.
29. O. B. Borisov, Yu. V. Dubinin, I. N. Zemskov *et al.*, *Sovremennaya diplomatiya burzhuaznykh gosudarstv* [The Contemporary Diplomacy of Bourgeois States] (Moscow: Izdatel'stvo Politcheskoy Literatury, 1981), p. 49. Dubinin is now the Soviet Ambassador to the United States.
30. N. N. Inozemtsev *et al.*, *Leninskaya teoriya imperializma*, p. 215.
31. Lebedev *et al.*, eds., *Mezhdunarodnye otnosheniya i bor'ba idei*, p. 8. This observation was made by V. V. Zagladin, candidate member of the Central Committee since 1976, deputy head of the International Department of the Central Committee from 1967 to 1988. See also Yevgeny Primakov, "Leninist Analysis of Imperialism and Contemporaneity," *Kommunist*, No. 9 (June 1986), as translated in Joint Publications Research Service, UKO-88-016, October 21, 1986, pp. 127–128; Elizabeth Kridl Valkenier, "New Soviet Thinking About the Third World," *World Policy Journal* 4, No. 4 (Fall 1987), pp. 651–674; and Viktor Yasmann, "The New Soviet Thinking and Regional Conflicts: Ideology and Politics," *Radio Liberty Research*, RD 493/87, December 3, 1987.

Moscow Conferences of Communist and Workers' Parties of 1957 and 1960, which declared that the world socialist system determined the principal content, direction and particularities in the historical evolution of human society.[32] (Consistent with the analysis given here, the 1969 Conference did not reiterate this point.) Rather, one has the impression of a world that, while less favorable to American interests than in the past, still presents impressive obstacles to the realization of Soviet designs. It is a world in which neither the Soviet Union nor the socialist countries together determine the main tendencies. "The imperialists," as the 1969 Conference noted, "impose on the developing countries economic agreements and military-political pacts which infringe upon their sovereignty; they exploit them through the export of capital, unequal terms of trade, manipulation of prices, exchange rates, loans and various forms of so-called aid and pressure from international financial organizations."[33]

Seventeen years later, in 1986, the new Soviet Party Program reaffirmed that multinational corporations, greatly strengthened as a result of "the capitalist concentration and internationalization of production . . . undermine the sovereignty of young states."[34] This is a world order from which the Soviet Union is essentially excluded, isolated in its own ghetto of satellite states. When the Soviet Union does affect this order, it is as often a disturber of it as collaborator in it, and it is certainly not, despite the rhetoric, the "determining" force in international relations. The successes it has achieved are defensive ones, securing first its right to exist and then recognition as a great power. At least, this is how it claims to see itself. When it challenges the existing order it is as an outsider, as one who does not contribute markedly to defining the rules and, as we have seen, deals from a weak position in relation to the main axes of world politics. The vision that is increasingly suggested by Soviet analyses of international relations, and

---

32. Cited in Brucan, *Dissolution of Power*, p. 138. For similar formulations see N. I. Lebedev, *SSSR v mirovoy politike* [The USSR in World Politics] (Moscow: Mezhdunarodnye Otnosheniya, 1980), p. 163, and A. V. Sergiyev, *Nauka i vneshnyaya politika* [Science and Foreign Policy] (Moscow: Znaniye, 1967), pp. 38, 39.
33. Cited in Brucan, *Dissolution of Power*, p. 10.
34. *Pravda*, March 7, 1986, as translated in FBIS, *Daily Report-Soviet Union (Supplement)*, March 10, 1986, p. 5.

which is rooted in views put forward in the late Brezhnev era, is that of a world which, from the standpoint of Soviet interests, is beginning to get somewhat out of control.[35] In an international system with Europe as the chief "arena," China as the chief security challenge, and the United States—occupying a favorable position in relation to both—as the chief global adversary, it is apparent that the Soviet Union is faced, and perceives itself as being faced, with an international system which both defies simple class analysis and is resistant to the easy extension of Soviet influence.[36]

This emerging Soviet vision of international relations is, consequently, a thoroughly political one. In itself this should hardly be surprising since "Leninism," in its internal, revolutionary aspect, represents above all a theory of political power, based on the institution of the political party. In this way Lenin went far beyond Marx's analysis of social class in his "recognition of politics as an autonomous field of activity . . ."[37] The Russian Revolution, unlike its bourgeois counterparts, a 1980 Soviet text on international relations theory reads, *started* with the political and accorded the political sphere primacy.[38] There is, then, a sound basis in communist theory for considering the primacy of politics, and thus of subjective (indeterminate) elements, in the analysis of international relations. Long forgotten and overlooked amidst the Marxist vocabulary of social class and the Stalinist assertion of the "two-camp doctrine," the Leninist *political* critique of revolution has survived to permeate contemporary Soviet writing on international relations.

The reemergence of the political critique in international analysis has had curious results for the Soviets. Soviet foreign-policy intellectuals now generally agree that the "subjective" political sphere exercises a strong influence on foreign policy, "thereby also influencing international economic and political relations." A. V. Grishin—son of ex-Politburo member Viktor Grishin—and his colleague N. M. Nikol'skiy have embraced

---

35. See V. V. Zagladin, "Predisloviye" [Introduction], in Lebedev *et al.*, *Mezhdunarodnye otnosheniya*, pp. 3–18.

36. Kokoshin, *S.Sh.A.*, pp. 20, 14–15; Appatov, *S.Sh.A. i Yevropa*, p. 5; Proyektor, *Puty Yevropa*, pp. 109–110, 112.

37. Samuel P. Huntington, *Political Order in Changing Societies* (New Haven: Yale University Press, 1968), p. 377. See Lenin's "What is to be Done?" in Robert C. Tucker, ed., *The Lenin Anthology* (New York: Norton, 1975), pp. 12–114.

38. Antyukhina-Moskovchenko *et al.*, *Osnovy teorii*, p. 71.

the notion of the dominance of the political sphere so thoroughly that they speak of "the reverse impact of economic, scientific and technological problems on international politics." Such problems as the arms race and arms control "cannot be defined by purely economic factors." In a contemporary discussion of Lenin's theory of imperialism, one Soviet analyst spoke of "the priority of politics over economics." Another has argued that, in respect of military detente, "everything in the final analysis depends on politics."[39] The greater weight assigned to subjective factors, in both the capitalist and socialist world, introduces the element of long-range indeterminacy into Soviet thinking. (While short-range indeterminacy had never been denied, it was always viewed in the context of the ultimate and not-too-distant triumph of socialism around the world.)

The Impact of Nuclear Weapons

The post-1956 interpretation of the impact of thermonuclear explosives introduced the possibility of temporal finality as well. As early as 1965, one Soviet analyst noted that nuclear-charged missiles presented "not only unlimited possibilities for offensive strikes against any target but the absolute impossibility of effective defense against such [nuclear] strikes." Other theorists, such as the junior Grishin, had argued that thermonuclear devices "have introduced qualitative changes in the posing of the problem of war and peace in the contemporary world." By threatening the very existence of civilization, nuclear explosives have eliminated the choice of general war as a means of attaining political objectives. This had led, Grishin wrote in 1982, to "the impossibility of preserving the institution of military victory in an unlimited, global, nuclear missile war."[40] The key factor here, according to Soviet

---

39. Sergiyev, *Nauka i vneshnyaya politika*, p. 25; Nikol'skiy and Grishin, *Nauchno-tekhnicheskiy progress*, pp. 283, 40; Kokoshin, *S.Sh.A.*, p. 42; Inozemtsev *et al., Leninskaya teoriya imperializma*, p. 331; *Problemy voyennoy razryadki* [Problems of Military Detente] (Moscow: Mezhdunarodnye Otnosheniya, 1981), p. 53.
40. V. I. Zamkovoy, *Kritika burzhuaznykh teoriy neizbezhnosti novoy mirovoy voyny* [A Critique of Bourgeois Theories of the Inevitability of a New World War] (Moscow: Mysl', 1965), p. 39; Grishin and Nikol'skiy, *Nauchno-tekhnicheskiy progress*, pp. 42, 263, 56, 47; Nikol'skiy and Grishin, *Sistemnyi analiz i dialog s EVM v issledovanii mezhdunarodnykh otnosheniy* [Systems Analysis and the Computer in International Relations Research]

analysts, is the existence of assured second-strike capabilities of both superpowers, which negates the political and thus military utility of nuclear devices and thereby the ability to effectively integrate them into political-strategic planning.[41]

Soviet analysts throughout the Brezhnev period approached the subject of actual nuclear warfare with great sobriety. Such warfare, IMEMO Director Nikolai Inozemtsev wrote, "is fraught with the annihilation . . . of the very conditions of human existence." The presence of such potentially suicidal weapons, which "do not observe the class principle," have altered something fundamental in the world historical process and "compel us all," noted journalist and spokesman Vladimir Lomeiko (one of the coiners of the phrase "new thinking"), "to new conceptions." "Clausewitz's formula," Fyodor Burlatsky has written, "whereby a big and powerful war corresponds to big politics does not 'work' in the conditions of thermonuclear warfare, since the greater the scope of such a war, the less will it be in the interests of big politics, insofar as the victors will be not better off than the vanquished."[42]

"The appearance of nuclear weapons," another Soviet observer has written, "accompanied by the never-ending growth in their power, the perfection of their technology and speed of their military employment, has led to the point where they have negated themselves and . . . have negated war as a means of resolving political problems of one sort or another." The classic relationship between offense and defense has thus been destroyed. "Many foreign researchers," Zamkovoy wrote, "underline not only the unlimited possibilities of offensive

---

(Moscow: Mezhdunarodnye Otnosheniya, 1982), p. 35. For a detailed account of Soviet views on nuclear war, including the views of both the professional military and the political leadership, see Mary C. Fitzgerald, *Changing Soviet Doctrine on Nuclear War* (Alexandria, Virginia: Center for Naval Analyses, CRM 86-234, October 1986).

41. Anatoly Gromyko (son of long-time foreign minister and later president Andrei Gromyko) and Vladimir Lomeiko, *Novoye myshleniye v yadernyi vek* [New Thinking in the Nuclear Age] (Moscow: Mezhdunarodnye Otnosheniya, 1984), pp. 9, 11, 17-18, 68, 163, 209, 230, 234.

42. Nikolai Inozemtsev, "Policy of Peaceful Coexistence: Underlying Principles," in *Soviet Policy of Peace* (Moscow: Social Sciences Today, 1979), pp. 19–20; Vladimir Lomeiko, "Predotvratit' yadernyi apokalipsis" [To Prevent a Nuclear Apocalypse], *Literaturnaya Gazeta*, August 29, 1979, back page; Fyodor Burlatsky, "Preventing World War and Planning Universal Peace," in *Soviet Policy of Peace*, p. 76.

strikes against any target but also the absolute impossibility of effective defense against such strikes."[43] Georgi Shakhnazarov argued that Clausewitz's dictum that war is the continuation of politics by other means must necessarily be questioned "when the sides confronting each other possess means of exterminating each other many times over . . . ." Whereas once, as Lenin noted, war served as the only reliable means of verifying the actual strength of states, thermonuclear weapons have put an end to this historical function of war. The increasing "dependence of the . . . class struggle . . . on the general correlation of class forces . . . in international relations," which themselves rest on the thermonuclear stalemate, signifies the elimination of global, now thermonuclear war, or the threat of such a war, as an agent of the world revolutionary process. Indeed, in such conditions revolution and progressive change are no longer to be accorded prior status as goals of the international proletariat. Instead, it is "the problem of preserving general peace and preventing a catastrophic conflict" that has been raised "to the level of Value Number One within any hierarchy of international values, regardless of the frame of reference in which it is considered." Nuclear war is thus to be conceived of as qualitatively different from all past wars.[44]

The historically unique, but apparently long-term revolution in military affairs that has been effected by nuclear energy in this way removes one element of the apparatus of coercion from the broad political function that Soviet analysts, civilian and military alike, have always attributed to military force. To be sure, nuclear weapons retain political significance, but it is difficult to imagine how they could be directly applied for political gain, especially before one side achieves a decisive superiority. Indeed, the very concept of military superiority, as traditionally understood, "loses its significance," according to the Soviet authors of a study of U.S. military-strategic ideas, "with the presence of the current enormous arsenals of nuclear

---

43. Zamkovoy, *Kritika burzhuaznykh teoriy*, pp. 40, 46; see also Grishin and Nikol'sky, *Nauchno-tekhnicheskiy progress*, pp. 42, 56.
44. Georgi Shakhnazarov, "The Problem of Peace: An Analysis of Basic Concepts," *The Soviet Review* 21, No. 3, p. 25; Inozemtsev *et al.*, eds., *Leninskaya teoriya imperializma i sovremennost'* [The Leninist Theory of Imperialism Today] (Moscow: Mysl', 1977), p. 25; Inozemtsev, "Policy of Peaceful Coexistence," pp. 7, 20; Burlatsky, "Preventing World War," pp. 74, 76.

weapons and the means of their delivery that have already been accumulated." Nuclear war, under such circumstances, must be considered to be excluded "as a means for achieving conceivable political objectives." On the one hand the United States would suffer an "unacceptable degree of damage . . . in such a war"; on the other hand, "even one-third of just [U.S.] SSBNs (i.e., submarine-based ballistic missiles) are capable of destroying twenty percent of the population and seventy-five percent of the industry of the Soviet Union." This condition of "assured destruction . . . which according to widely held opinion expresses the actual situation at the moment," reduces the function of strategic nuclear weapons to the deterrence of their use by one's opponent. It is difficult to envisage a more ambitious purpose for these arms because "no policy can posit as its goal the elimination of an opponent at the price of its own complete destruction." A widening gap has thus developed between the power of military force and the opportunities for its use: how is one to deal with "the extremely narrow borders of the possibility of the . . . application" of thermonuclear weapons?[45]

Most importantly, the presence and current distribution of nuclear weapons transforms the desirability of avoiding a global conflict into a real possibility. The very destructiveness of atomic warfare, which now raises the possibility of destroying "ten-tenths" of humanity, tends to insure against its occurrence. Such a possibility, which had been anticipated by the Soviet political economist Yevgeny Varga in 1953, transforms the very meaning of force in international relations, resulting in a "diminution in the role and significance of the purely military functions of strategy . . . ." The development of strategic nuclear weapons systems in the 1960s and 1970s had the effect "of ensuring mutual deterrence and probably even of increasing its reliability . . . . [I]t created a situation of strategic

45. Institut S.Sh.A. i Kanadi, *S.Sh.A.: Voyenno-strategicheskiye kontseptsii* [U.S. Military-strategic Concepts] (Moscow: Nauka, 1980), pp. 298, 178, 10, 6; G.I. Svyatov, "Grand Strategy," *U.S.A.*, no. 8 (August 1975), p. 93 (Joint Publications Research Service [J.P.R.S.] translation); Michael A. Milstein and Leo S. Semeiko, "Problems of the Inadmissability of Nuclear Conflict," *International Studies Quarterly* 20, No. 1 (March 1976), p. 98; V. I. Gantman, ed., *Sovremennye burzhuaznye teorii mezhdunarodnykh otnosheniy* [Contemporary Bourgeois Theories of International Relations] (Moscow: Nauka, 1976), p. 6.

deadlock which has so far helped to avert a nuclear conflict. Despite destabilizing trends in certain areas, such as the development of nuclear missiles with multiple warheads, which seem to make nuclear war more purely military, more selective in nature, the multiplicity of responses available to each superpower ensures that the stability of "the bilateral Soviet-American [strategic] balance will not undergo essential changes. . . ."[46]

This "dynamic stability" of the nuclear balance brings substantial weight to bear upon the foreign policies of both superpowers, for it tends to sever the link between interstate relations and international social development as well as that between war and revolution. The issue in such circumstances is not the rational, calculated start of nuclear war, for that is "obviously suicidal." The danger, rather, lies in the "escalation" of tension and conflict from areas peripheral to the immediate interests of the superpowers to a military confrontation between them. The element of chance in such conditions, leading, conceivably, to a nuclear confrontation where irrationality might play an important part, requires that the United States and the Soviet Union avoid political confrontations of all kinds and seek to "manage" those that do arise. The stable character of the strategic balance between the superpowers now provides the opportunity for quarantining the "essential" economic, political, and ideological struggle of the United States and the Soviet Union—as leaders of the socioeconomic *systems* of capitalism and socialism—from their relations as *states.*[47]

---

46. F. V. Konstantinov *et al., Kritika teoreticheskikh kontseptsiy Mao Tsze-duna* [A Critique of the Theoretical Conceptions of Mao Tse-Tung] (Moscow: Mysl', 1970), pp. 113, 116; Zamkovoy, *Kritika burzhuaznykh teoriy,* p. 6; Yevgeny Varga, *Osnovnye voprosy ekonomiki i politiki imperializma* [Main Issues in the Economy and Policy of Imperialism] (Moscow: Politicheskaya Literatura, 1953), p. 155; A. D. Nikonov, "Sovremennaya revolyutsiya vo voyennom dele" [The Contemporary Revolution in Military Affairs], *Mirovaya Ekonomika i Mezhdunarodnye Otnosheniya,* No. 2 (February 1969), p. 14; Georgy Arbatov (Director of the Institute on U.S. and Canada Studies and a full Central Committee member), "Detente and the Problem of Conflict," in *Soviet Policy of Peace,* pp. 37–38; G. A. Trofimenko, "Evolyutsiya amerikanskoy voyenno-politicheskoy mysli" [The Evolution of U.S. Military-political Thinking], in Trofimenko, ed., *Sovremennye vneshne-politicheskiye kontseptsii S.Sh.A.* [Contemporary U.S. Foreign Policy Concepts] (Moscow: Nauka, 1979), pp. 124, 126, 128.
47. Arbatov, "Detente and the Problem of Conflict," pp. 34–35.

The Character of Western Capitalism

Finally, there has been a very heightened appreciation by Soviet foreign-policy analysts of the underlying stability and dynamism of capitalism in the West. Pessimism over the revolutionary potential of the Western proletariat is in fact deeply rooted in the Bolshevik tradition. Lenin himself felt compelled to advance the thesis of "superprofits," derived from colonial exploitation and divided among a worker aristocracy, to explain the "docility" of the Western working class. Contemporary Soviet analysts expand upon the early postwar work of political economist Yevgeny Varga and admit the high level of economic growth attained in the West after the war, while others have observed that such efforts as the European Economic Community have far surpassed the limits anticipated by their initiators. "Present-day capitalism," the 1986 Party Program states, "differs in many respects from what it was . . . even in the middle of the twentieth century." "The natural course of events," Vadim Zagladin, ex-chief of the Central Committee's International Department, has thus observed, "is not going to make capitalism collapse." What is more, the late Soviet leader Konstantin Chernenko declared in April 1984 that contemporary capitalism "still possesses quite substantial and far from exhausted reserves for development."[48] There is a broadly shared consensus among Soviet political analysts and leaders that the flexibility of "production relations" in the capitalist economies has led to greater economic opportunities and to a certain degree of social compromise among classes. The strengthened position of multinational corporations, assisted by the role of state economic regulation, has, in this view (which has its roots in the postwar Varga controversy), enabled capitalism to adjust to and exploit the opportunities offered by the scientific-technical revolution. (This applies to Third World countries as well, many of whom are seen to be doing quite well economically. For more, see pp. 48–49.)[49]

---

48. Lenin, *Imperialism*, p. 12; Inozemtsev *et al.*, *Leninskaya teoriya imperializma*, p. 435; Zagladin quote in Lebedev *et al.*, *Mezhdunarodnye otnosheniya*, p. 137; FBIS, *Daily Report-Soviet Union. (Supplement)*, March 10, 1986, p. 5; *Pravda*, April 25, 1984, p. 1.
49. Primakov, "Leninist Analysis," pp. 118–123, 127–28.

■ The Legacy of Brezhnev-Era Analysis

Thus, by the end of the Brezhnev era, many of the postulates that had dominated the Stalin and even Khrushchev years had begun to be challenged and reshaped by Soviet analysts and theoreticians. These modifications laid the conceptual basis for many of the changes that have taken place over the past four years under Gorbachev. The most important of these modifications were related to the indeterminacy of world politics, the possibility of general annihilation through nuclear war, and the underlying stability and creative dynamism of the capitalist West. The cumulative effect has been to sever the link between world war and revolution, thereby effecting a progressive "de-utopianization" of Soviet thinking about international relations.

In fact, this development has deeper roots in Soviet history. Very shortly after the Russian Revolution one could detect a tendency among Soviet leaders to steadily elongate their expectations about the coming of communism from a few years to several generations to half a century or more.[50] "After the mid-1920s," Elliot Goodman writes, "the game of predicting the exact date for the arrival of stateless communism appears to have gone out of fashion."[51] By the Brezhnev period, Soviet commentators were speaking of "entire historical epochs," lasting centuries, as the time for the transition to communism on a global scale, in effect placing the ultimate objective at the end of time, thereby depriving it of operational significance for the conduct of Soviet foreign policy.[52]

In certain respects, then, the professional Soviet analysis of world politics, as developed throughout the Brezhnev period, did display signs of diverging from traditional Leninist assumptions. International relations were increasingly seen as an open-ended phenomenon, with no fixed destination. World politics were now held to be dominated by states, not classes,

---

50. Lenin said in March 1918 that the withering-away of the state would have to wait until "at least two more Party Congresses" had passed. Bukharin declared in the following year that "two or three generations" might have to go by before the coming of communism. In that same year (1919) Lenin was now speaking of thirty to forty years, while Stalin, in 1925, mentioned "an entire historical era" as the period necessary for the transition to communism. Elliot R. Goodman, *Soviet Design for a World State* (New York: Columbia University Press, 1960), pp. 448–449.

51. Ibid., p. 449.

52. Inozemtsev *et al.*, *Leninskaya teoriya imperializma*, pp. 15, 19.

and the constituent states may be said to constitute a system that is more than the sum of its parts. Political considerations, emanating chiefly, though not exclusively, from their position in the interstate system, dominate the foreign-policy calculations of these states.[53] General war, though no longer inevitable, may now be universally fatal and so must be expunged from the course of world politics. Finally, revolution, at least revolution according to the Bolshevik model, is not on the agenda—first of all because of the fundamental stability of the capitalist countries and second because thermonuclear weapons cannot be employed as its handmaiden.

In sum, the preceding analysis of the post-Stalin Soviet study of international relations shows that the original Leninist deduction of international-political behavior from the class character of specific states, projecting, as George Liska has noted, "the alleged internal contradictions of capitalism onto the international arena,"[54] had by the end of the Brezhnev period been qualified in so many ways that its operational significance for Soviet theorists—and policy-makers—may be seriously questioned. Certainly the bitter dispute with communist Yugoslavia after 1948, and especially the Sino-Soviet schism, are inexplicable by a theory which ascribes the wellspring of all "antagonistic" contradictions to inter-class struggle. Soviet analysts seem to have grasped the implications of this theoretical impasse. They responded to the confrontation with communist China not by denying the class essence of the People's Republic, but by claiming that a gang of renegades had acquired control of the state apparatus and was executing a reactionary, pro-imperialist foreign policy.

The series of challenges posed by the Chinese communists to the Soviet Union ever since the late 1950s appears to have moved Soviet analysts to clarify their own thinking about the moving forces in world politics in a number of fundamental ways. In the first place, Chinese insistence in the 1950s that the Soviet Union place its nuclear force at the disposal of Chinese foreign policy—in particular in its dispute with the United States over the offshore islands of Quemoy and Matsu—led the

---

53. Kokoshin, *S.Sh.A.*, pp. 4, 5, 6–7, 8, 74–75, 338–339, 341; Usachev, *Mezhdunarodnaya razryadka*, p. 4.
54. George Liska, *Russia and World Order* (Baltimore: Johns Hopkins University Press, 1980), p. 141.

Soviet Union formally to distinguish sharply between the national interests of the Soviet Union and China and their nominal class solidarity. In support of their position, the Soviet leaders advanced the thesis that the catastrophic consequences of nuclear war nullified any gains to be won by the annihilation of capitalism. Furthermore, responding to Chinese taunts for a more aggressive Soviet global posture, Khrushchev argued that international conditions had changed so much that global war was no longer an inevitability.

Over time, as the ideological dispute between the Soviet and Chinese communist parties grew into a political and then military confrontation between the two states, Soviet theorists were led to admit explicitly the possibility of war between communist countries. By itself, the Soviet response to the split with China brought into question and dealt a decisive blow to such critical Leninist tenets as the predominance of class as opposed to national factors in explaining international behavior; the inevitability of war in an international environment riven by class schism; and the impossibility of war between communist states. The fact that the schism with China largely parallels the development of international studies in the Soviet Union, and especially the progressive divergence from essential Leninist formulations on world politics, is surely a telling one. For although many of the tendencies examined here have roots independent of the Sino-Soviet split, the split has certainly encouraged Soviet theorists to develop the implications of their heresies to a far fuller extent than would otherwise have been the case. In practical terms, the Soviet experience with China convincingly refutes the easy Soviet (and Western) assumption that the expansion of communism internationally is perforce consistent with Soviet national interests. This key Bolshevik tenet, which had first been challenged by Tito's defiance of Stalin in 1948, could no longer be squared with the character of change in a world driven by contemporary nationalism.

3

The Gorbachev Synthesis: Elements of the "New Thinking"

In forging the "new political thinking," Gorbachev, together with his advisors—many with close personal and professional links to the foreign-policy intellectuals—has drawn upon the conceptual spade work done during the Brezhnev and Andropov periods and adapted it to his basic foreign-policy priorities. In part, this is designed to make more persuasive, to both domestic and foreign audiences, the new course that Gorbachev has set himself in foreign affairs, which is aimed at launching a broad international detente as both context and catalyst of reform at home (unlike the Brezhnev detente, which in many ways served, via expanded trade and technology transfer, as a substitute for meaningful domestic reform). Encouragement of a relatively freewheeling debate is also aimed at provoking responses and internal debate from normally reticent quarters, such as the military, and so to raise issues and elicit information that the political leadership requires in making effective national decisions. Furthermore, Gorbachev evidently finds the global vision offered by the "new thinkers" a more persuasive analysis than the one inherited from his predecessors, which had in all too many instances led the USSR into burdensome arms races and international isolation. Certainly, the party leadership has not spared the foreign-policy vision of the Brezhnev era from the withering criticism of *glasnost'* (see epigraph on p. 1). Most important, however, the "new political thinking" represents a determined effort by the Soviet leadership to redefine the nature of the threat environment facing the USSR and in the process monopolize domestic Soviet discussion of the future military, economic and political agenda of the Soviet state. In this respect, the "new political thinking" cannot be divorced from the economic crisis of the Soviet system.

In many ways, the world view that Gorbachev and his colleagues have been formulating represents an explicit crystallization of tendencies that have been present—albeit often in piecemeal form—in Soviet policy circles since Nikita Khrushchev's anti-Stalin speech at the Twentieth Party Congress in 1956. The resultant synthesis constitutes a distinctly "Gorbachevian" perspective, reflected most dramatically in the statements of the general secretary himself, which seek to integrate foreign and domestic policy in a mutually reinforcing combination. This synthesis may be summarized as follows:

First, the Soviet leadership has concluded, and repeatedly made explicit to both foreign and domestic audiences, that the USSR's international relationships are not to be a distraction from, and wherever possible a positive inducement to, the prime task of economic modernization at home. "The main thing," Soviet Foreign Minister Eduard Shevardnadze (another strong exponent of the "new thinking") said in a speech to the Soviet diplomatic community in June 1987, "is that our country not incur additional expenses in conjunction with the need to maintain its defense capacity and protect its legitimate foreign-policy interests. This means," Shevardnadze went on to say:

> that we must seek ways to limit and reduce military rivalry, eliminate confrontational features in relations with other states, and suppress conflict and crisis situations.[55]

The logic of Gorbachev's policy of domestic reform has led the Soviet leader to begin searching for structures of stability in critical areas—in arms control most visibly, and now international organizations as well—so as to provide a durable and predictable framework for the resource choices that must be made in the coming decade and beyond. The need for such stability assumes double importance for Gorbachev since instability in the USSR's foreign relations will affect not only the politics of resource allocation but the viability of Gorbachev's own political position, which assumes that far-reaching reform

---

55. See Shevardnadze's candid speech to the Soviet foreign-policy community in *Vestnik Ministerstva Inostrannykh Del SSSR*, No. 2 (1987), pp. 30–34, in which Shevardnadze clearly sets forth the priority of internal economic development in all of the USSR's foreign relationships.

at home is consistent with the USSR's geopolitical presence abroad.

Second, the Gorbachev leadership has apparently come to the conclusion that a favorable international environment can only be created on a *political* basis with the leading industrial powers, and above all with the United States. With remarkable tenacity, Gorbachev has sought to strike a *modus vivendi* with the United States, which is the key toward establishing predictability in the USSR's foreign affairs and security requirements and would translate into a major victory for Gorbachev at home. The Soviet choice for detente thus represents more than a "tactical" adjustment to shifting circumstances, the "breathing spell" that some in the West have detected, and reflects a strategic and realistic reevaluation of the international environment—based on dealing with established governments in the advanced industrial world—and of the USSR's position in relation to that environment.

Third, there has been a major reexamination of security issues, led by the official confirmation by Gorbachev *and* the Soviet military that a nuclear war cannot under any circumstances be won. "The time has come," Mikhail Gorbachev said in his Political Report to the Twenty-Seventh Soviet Party Congress, "to realize thoroughly the harsh realities of our day: nuclear weapons harbor a hurricane which is capable of sweeping the human race from the face of the earth."[56] As a corollary, the leadership now argues, with implicit criticism of Soviet security policy under Brezhnev, that security cannot be obtained through military means alone. Security in the nuclear age is said to be mutual in character and, due to the destructive potential of modern weaponry, a common concern of all countries. Relatedly, Soviet policy analysts and Gorbachev himself reject nuclear weapons as a durable guarantor of peace. They claim that even nuclear parity, which they continue to regard as a major historical achievement of socialism, could cease to be a determining factor for stability in the face of an unregulated arms competition between East and West. Nuclear arms control thus assumes priority as a means of reducing the external threat, limiting resource requirements for the military, and establishing a framework of stability in East-West

---

56. Mikhail Gorbachev, *Political Report of the CPSU Central Committee to the 27th Party Congress* (Moscow: Novosti, 1986), p. 78.

strategic relations. In Europe, Gorbachev has apparently come to the conclusion that, in principle, the USSR cannot secure a significant further diminution of NATO's nuclear presence on the continent without at the same time addressing the issue of its own conventional posture and operational doctrine. Toward this end, Gorbachev has admitted the need to reduce "asymmetries" in the conventional arms balance in Europe, thereby admitting the problem posed by Soviet superiority in forward-based tank forces for further arms control in Europe. Most dramatically, in December 1988 he announced a unilateral reduction of Soviet forces by 500,000 men and the intention of making the remaining forces unmistakably defensive in orientation. Negotiating on this recognition, however, will prove complex in the extreme.[57] It should be seen as a starting point for serious discussion of the central military issue in East-West relations—the political role of armed force in the heart of Europe—rather than as a sign of impending movement in conventional arms control.

Fourth, the Soviet concept of peaceful coexistence is being revised. Key Soviet policy analysts and officials now interpret peaceful coexistence less as a form of class struggle—the traditional Soviet viewpoint—and more as a long-lasting condition in which states with different social and political systems will have to learn how to live with each other for the indefinite future. As Yevgeny Primakov, head of the international relations section of the Academy of Sciences and a close advisor to Gorbachev, noted in a key article in *Pravda* in the summer of 1987, peaceful coexistence is no longer regarded "as a breathing space" by the Soviets. "Interstate relations," he emphasized, "cannot be the sphere in which the outcome of the confrontation between world socialism and world capitalism is settled."[58] Such "active" coexistence is said to imply not simply the absence of war but instead an international order in which not military strength but relations of confidence and cooperation prevail and "global problems"—the arms race, ecological problems, Third World development—can be

---

57. For details, see Joachim Krause, *Prospects for Conventional Arms Control in Europe* (New York: Institute for East-West Security Studies, Occasional Paper No. 8, 1988).
58. "Novaya filosofiya vneshnei politiki" [A New Philosophy of Foreign Policy], *Pravda,* July 10, 1987, p. 4. See also Primakov, "Leninist Analysis," p. 128.

resolved on a collaborative basis. Gorbachev has written that the Soviet leadership has "taken the steps necessary to rid our policy of ideological prejudice."[59] If this in fact leads to a more pragmatic understanding of peaceful coexistence, with "class interests" strictly subordinate to geopolitical criteria in the daily conduct of foreign policy, a central obstacle to more genuinely collaborative East-West relations would have been removed. Certainly, it would mean that the United States and the Soviet Union might actually agree on the operational significance of "normal" relations, which proved impossible during the detente of the early 1970s. "New rules of coexistence," as Gorbachev put it in a key article on September 17, 1987 (reported to have been drafted by Deputy Foreign Minister Petrovsky), might then be drawn up.[60] Soviet officials, both pro- and contra-Gorbachev, have themselves recognized the centrality of this point for the integrity of Gorbachev's foreign and domestic policy vision and program. Speaking to the Soviet diplomatic community after the June party conference, Foreign Minister Shevardnadze explicitly declared the second-rank order of ideological/class values in contemporary Soviet foreign policy. In the words of the TASS account of Shevardnadze's speech:

> ... the new political thinking views peaceful coexistence in the realities of the nuclear century. We are fully justified in refusing to see in it a special form of class struggle. One must not identify coexistence ... with class struggle. The struggle between two opposing systems is no longer a determining tendency of the present-day era.[61]

The implications of Shevardnadze's remarks were underscored with dramatic effect when Yegor Ligachev, at the time the "second secretary" of the CPSU, joined the issue in early August in the first open challenge to Gorbachev's foreign-policy vision. At the end of a speech on domestic affairs, in which he again cast scorn on market-oriented reforms, Ligachev suddenly turned to foreign policy and declared: "We

---

59. Mikhail S. Gorbachev, *Perestroika: New Thinking for Our Country and the World* (New York: Harper & Row, 1987), p. 250.
60. For Gorbachev's article, entitled "The Reality and Guarantees of a Secure World," see *Pravda*, September 17, 1987, pp. 1–2, translated in FBIS, *Daily Report-Soviet Union*, FBIS-SOV-87–180, September 17, 1987, pp. 23–28.
61. *Pravda*, July 26, 1988, p. 4, as translated in *FBIS-SU*, July 26, 1988, p. 30.

proceed from the class nature of international relations. Any other formulation of the issue only introduces confusion into the thinking of Soviet people and our friends abroad. Active involvement in the solution of general human problems by no means signifies any artificial 'braking' of the social and national liberation struggle."[62] Having earlier failed to curb the scope of Gorbachev's reforms on domestic grounds, Ligachev seems to have turned to foreign policy, where he may have hoped to find a more receptive audience. He evidently saw foreign policy as the "weak link" in Gorbachev's strategy: by attacking foreign policy reform, domestic reform might also be scaled down and vested party interests respected.

That the leadership is sensitive to the interdependence between foreign and domestic policy is shown by Gorbachev ally Alexandr Yakovlev's quick and brisk defense of the new foreign-policy line several days later, when he reiterated the subordination of class interests to "all-human" interests such as survival in the nuclear age. At issue is the right to define the nature of the threat environment facing the USSR, and thus the nature and level of the Soviet political and military response to it. If "class" values remain paramount, then the threat from the class enemy remains high and the USSR cannot afford the relative diminution of Soviet military expenditures, the (again relative) demilitarization of Soviet foreign policy—especially in the Third World—and therefore the reorientation of political values implied by Gorbachev's domestic economic reform. In this way, a debate over arcana of ideology is really a struggle for the acceptable framework of choice in reform, in both foreign and domestic policy, and bears directly on the prospects for reform at home. It is thus not coincidental that on October 4, 1988, shortly after Gorbachev's "purge" of the top leadership, the new party secretary for ideology, Vadim Medvedev, should issue a ringing defense of the Gorbachev line on this point. (Needless to say, removal of the current leadership, a prospect made more unlikely by the evident demotion of Yegor Ligachev in late September 1988, would in turn have important foreign-policy consequences).[63]

---

62. *Pravda*, August 6, 1988, p. 2, as translated in *FBIS-SU*, August 8, 1988, p. 39.
63. Central Television, August 12, 1988, as cited in Elizabeth Teague, "Kremlin Leaders at Loggerheads," *Radio Liberty Research*, August 16, 1988, p. 5. For Medvedev's remarks see *Pravda*, October 5, 1988, p. 5.

Finally, the Gorbachev leadership evidences increasing recognition of the multipolar and interdependent character of contemporary international relations. This view has been reflected in a Soviet tendency to deal directly with key regional actors, such as China and Japan in the Far East, Egypt and Israel in the Middle East, and Mexico in Central America. The West can expect increasingly sophisticated and pragmatic Soviet policies throughout the world, as Soviet diplomacy seeks both to reduce the isolation which the rigidity of the late Brezhnev era—with its "excessive devotion to ideology" and its near obsession with the United States—had at times forced upon the USSR and to multiply Soviet options.[64] (The rapid resolution of the Swedish sea boundary dispute in January 1988, after two decades of deadlock, may be seen in this light.)

Gorbachev's November 2, 1987, speech commemorating the seventieth anniversary of the Bolshevik Revolution included a synthesis of the many analytical and political tendencies discussed in this paper.[65] The development of nuclear weapons, Gorbachev said, by threatening "the very survival of the human race," has led to a redefinition of the Leninist concept of peaceful coexistence, which had originally been designed to buy time for the young Soviet state to build up its strength. But the global interdependence underlined in starkest form by nuclear weapons has caused a shift in the concept of peaceful coexistence from an instrument of the international class struggle to "a condition for the survival of the entire human race." Gorbachev directly links this conceptual shift to the idea of "reasonable sufficiency" as the criterion for NATO and Warsaw Pact military forces and to the strengthening and better utilization of the United Nations to assist "a balance of interests of all countries and to discharge its peacemaking functions effectively." (In the entire international section of the report, there is only one sentence devoted to defense issues, and that simply discusses the need to prevent "imperialism" from achieving military superiority.)

---

64. See the *Pravda* interview with Soviet diplomat Aleksandr Belonogov, in which Belonogov—the Soviet permanent representative at the UN—criticized the conduct of Soviet foreign policy during Gromyko's tenure as foreign minister. *Pravda*, October 3, 1988.
65. The following quotes from Gorbachev's speech come from the TASS English translation provided by the Soviet Embassy to the United States, "October and Perestroika: The Revolution Continues," pp. 39–55. (See Appendix.)

Elsewhere in the speech, Gorbachev reaffirms the recent official Soviet recognition of the basic stability, and even dynamism, of the West. "The changes occurring within the technological and organizational infrastructure of the capitalist economy," he notes, "also helped to allay contradictions and to balance different interests." His discussion of inter-socialist relations proceeds from the recognition of specific national interests under socialism and reflects some humility as regards the general applicability of the Soviet model of development, even to its Warsaw Pact neighbors:

> Life has corrected our notions of the laws and rates of transition to socialism, our understanding of the role of socialism on the world scale.[66]

Curiously, Gorbachev argues that "the practice of socialist internationalism rests on . . . a strict observance of the principles of peaceful coexistence by all." Does the application of the concept of peaceful coexistence—which has previously applied only to "class-antagonistic" states—to intra-bloc affairs signify a move toward a more normal relationship between the Soviet Union and Eastern Europe? This will bear close watching, since such a formulation actually provided a basis for the normalization of Sino-Soviet state-to-state relations in the 1980s (even while party relations remain frozen).

The revised Soviet estimate of prospects for socialist change and Soviet influence in the Third World also found expression in Gorbachev's speech. Noting references to "the decline of the national liberation movement" (which he admitted was "certainly waning"), Gorbachev paints a complex and pessimistic picture. Factors making for progressive impulses in the Third World are "varied and far from simple" and should not "yield to pessimism," though it is clear from the whole tone of the analysis that prospects for quick Soviet influence are dim. Indeed, Gorbachev refers to a time span of fifty years, during which it is difficult to predict developments. As with the West and even Soviet allies, Gorbachev alludes to the frustration of earlier Soviet hopes for the applicability of the Soviet model: the Third World, he says, "is a world of its own . . . ."

---

66. For background on the internal discussion on the character of Soviet-East European relations, see Lynch, *The Soviet Study of International Relations*, pp. 115–124.

Most remarkably, Gorbachev raises a series of questions in his speech that go to the heart of the traditional Leninist conception of international politics. These include:

- Is it possible to influence the (aggressive) nature of imperialism and block its more dangerous manifestations? (Gorbachev leaves the question unanswered.)
- "Can capitalism get rid of militarism and function and develop in the economic sphere without it?" (He suggests the answer is yes.)
- "Can the capitalist system do without neocolonialism, which is currently one of the factors essential to its survival?" (Here too he suggests that the answer is yes: "the situation does not seem to defy resolution; "contradictions can be modified.")
- Will the awareness of the nuclear threat that "is making its way even into the higher echelons of the Western ruling elite . . . be translated into practical policies?" (Unanswered.)

Simply to raise such ideologically charged questions, not to mention answering in the affirmative, implicitly challenges central Leninist tenets on the nature of imperialism and the wellsprings of conflict in world politics. The debate over the nature of imperialism, i.e., whether it can be restrained only by external (Soviet) power or by forces intrinsic to it ("bourgeois democracy"), has fundamental implications for the kind of external threat said to be facing the USSR. If imperialism can be contained by internal forces, then the requirements on Soviet security policy (and defense spending) are reduced accordingly. That Gorbachev has raised these questions in this way, and provided even partial answers, shows that the new flexibility in Soviet rhetoric and policy reflects a fundamental reevaluation of the relationship between the Soviet Union and its external environment. Taken together, and in light of the analytical background with its roots in the Brezhnev and Khrushchev periods, one may even speak of the emergence, as yet hesitant and partial, of a new Soviet theory of international relations.

4

Motive Forces: Impact of the International System

The discussion of the Khrushchev and Brezhnev periods shows that three key developments were behind the shift in Soviet foreign policy perspectives from a strict Leninist analytical orthodoxy to a more pragmatic, geo-politically oriented critique: the universal threat of nuclear weapons; the continued prosperity and stability of the West; and the emergence of a communist China as perhaps the key security challenge to the USSR. Yet clearly, these developments in themselves did not compel Soviet policy-makers to undertake the kind of fundamental reevaluation of Soviet foreign-policy priorities and objectives as that now being done by the Gorbachev leadership. What happened to cause the Gorbachev leaders to declare the inadequacy of Brezhnev-era foreign policy?

Over time, beginning in the late 1970s, other factors, rooted in the international system, further challenged basic Soviet assumptions about the international order. These included:

- the increased technological creativity and dynamism of the capitalist West, which has led to the information revolution and an ever increasing economic gap with the West;
- the intractability of change in the Third World, together with the fact that since the late 1970s the USSR has found itself in the position of propping up threatened regimes in Angola, Afghanistan, Cambodia, etc.;
- a further structural shift in power relations in international politics, with a decrease in superpower influence, particularly within their own alliance systems;
- a qualitatively greater degree of international interdependence, which refutes the purely "zero sum" (*kto-kogo*) view of

international relations and highlights the impact of forms of power other than that of armed force; and

- the consequences of nuclear parity, i.e., given the obvious limits to the political use of nuclear weapons, what kind of military policy should the USSR have under conditions of both a continuing arms race and nuclear parity?

No doubt, specific events also played a role in this analysis, especially the change of political atmosphere in Moscow that enabled the "new thinkers" to find a more receptive audience at the top. A general analysis of recent trends in Soviet foreign policy, supported by the author's discussions with specialists inside the USSR, indicates at least four key developments which served to shake given assumptions about the way the USSR conducts its international relationships.

First, the invasion and then stalemate in Afghanistan served to accelerate a reevaluation by the top leadership of the role of ideological considerations and of military-technical criteria in the definition of security interests and the formulation of security policy and foreign policy more generally. While it would be wrong at this point to generalize from the specific Soviet decision to withdraw from Afghanistan to the character of Soviet security interests in Eastern Europe, the Afghan fiasco has put a very heavy burden of proof upon those within the Soviet system arguing for military solutions to ideological challenges. "There was," the Soviet journalist (and long-time vocal supporter of the war effort) Aleksandr Prokhanov has written about the Soviet decision to invade, "an incorrect analysis of the situation. The experts evaluating the situation in the country were wrong. The specialists on Islam, the diplomats, the politicians, and the military, were wrong."[67] (Interestingly, Prokhanov does not include the intelligence services, i.e., the KGB—at the time headed by Yury Andropov—among those guilty of mistaken judgment.) That this reflects long-term considerations is shown by Gorbachev's reference to Afghanistan as a "bleeding wound" at the 27th Party Congress in February 1986, i.e., well before the famous Stinger anti-aircraft missiles had begun to make an impact upon Soviet power-projection capabilities within Afghanistan.

---

67. Aleksandr Prokhanov, "Afganskiye voprosy" [Afghan Questions], *Literaturnaya Gazeta*, No. 7 (February 18, 1988), p. 9.

Second, the advent of the Reagan administration surprised both leadership and specialists in their assumptions about the limits of hostility in contemporary U.S.-Soviet relations. A leading Soviet Americanist has recently written that "the opposition of the extreme right, and of the right [to detente], in the American establishment, turned out to be much more stubborn and broad-based than was possible to foresee."[68] The disarray of an increasingly immobile regime's received wisdom about relations with the chief adversary was further compounded by NATO's successful deployment of U.S. intermediate-range nuclear missiles after November 1983. Traditional Soviet ways of countering U.S. pressure, i.e., by appealing over the heads of governments to populations and attempting to play both halves of NATO against the other, were clearly not working. What was to be done?

Third, the promulgation of the Strategic Defense Initiative in March 1983 appears to have encouraged a reevaluation of the concept of military-nuclear parity (and by extension of defense sufficiency) by plausibly (to Soviet observers at the time) threatening the political significance of the USSR's accumulated investment in nuclear-charged ballistic missiles. Initially, many Soviet observers embraced (for the first time) the *desirability* of the condition of mutual assured destruction for the medium term, and later began to question the relationship between the parity and stability.[69]

Fourth, and hardly to be underestimated, the Soviet leadership took full measure of the economic crisis facing the Soviet system (euphemistically termed "pre-crisis phenomena" by Gorbachev). This is—probably—not a crisis of the survival of socialism, but rather of the USSR's capacity to meet its domestic and foreign-policy objectives. At the ideological plenum of the

---

68. Podlesnyi in Trofimenko and Podlesnyi, eds., *Sovetsko-amerikanskiye otnosheniya*, p. 106. See also the discussion and sources cited in Stephen Shenfield, *The Nuclear Predicament. Explorations in Soviet Ideology* (London: Routledge & Kegan Paul, Chatham House Papers No. 37, 1987), pp. 30–39.

69. By the mid-1970s, the Soviet leadership had come to recognize mutual assured destruction as an existential condition of East-West strategic relations. They had not, as some U.S. theorists and statesmen had, recognized it as a *desirable* condition. In response to the proclamation of SDI, one began to detect the idea that mutual assured destruction is a desirable condition to preserve, at least in relation to the alternative of the negation of mutual deterrence through SDI.

Central Committee on February 18, 1988, Gorbachev said that, omitting as non-productive factors the sales of oil abroad and of alcohol at home from calculations of growth, "practically over four five-year plan periods there was no increase in the absolute increment of the national income, and it even began declining in the early eighties."[70] That is, for nearly a quarter-century the Soviet economy suffered from progressively decreasing growth rates and then, in the early 1980s, plunged into a de facto depression (in an economy which never mastered the first industrial revolution!).

This accumulation of trends and events, both internal and external, has led to a serious discrediting of the traditional ideological school of "scientific communism" within the USSR, of its ability and reputation to provide an adequate conceptual framework for understanding and anticipating developments. Perhaps we may even speak of a crisis of explanatory conceptual "paradigms," in the sense used by the historian of science Thomas Kuhn as he tried to explain conceptual revolutions in science.[71] In the process, an opportunity has been offered to specialists in international relations and other fields to step into the breach and provide the leadership with a new framework for dealing with the USSR's myriad problems of domestic and foreign policy. The immediate result has been the launching of a fundamental revision in the way that the Soviet leadership claims to see the basic trends in world politics and their implications for the USSR, i.e., the "new political thinking." That such a revision has come about as a result of a certain process of adaptation by the Soviet political system to the outside world (and vice versa) says much about the potential adaptability of the Soviet system and, indeed, about the wellsprings of Soviet foreign policy.

---

70. Mikhail Gorbachev, *The Ideology of Renewal for Revolutionary Restructuring* (Moscow: Novosti, 1988), p. 36.
71. See Thomas Kuhn, *The Structure of Scientific Revolutions* (Chicago: University of Chicago Press, 1970, 2nd ed.). See also Shenfield, *The Nuclear Predicament*, especially the chapter entitled "The Orthodoxy in Crisis."

5

New Parameters of Discussion

The advent of the "new political thinking" in the USSR has in effect "liberated" a whole series of analytical positions which had previously been limited to discussions among (often like-minded) specialists and catapulted these views and their adherents into the forefront of the contemporary Soviet political debate. In the process, the authors of revisionist interpretations of foreign policy and international relations have found themselves publicly developing their positions further than they perhaps realized possible. In every case, a political impulse from above has been required to set this process in motion, but once under way it has acquired a certain autonomous character, going beyond bounds which the leadership perhaps originally envisioned. A brief review of developments in three areas, corresponding to the main lines of conceptual revision begun in the Brezhnev period—the role of ideology in foreign policy, the place of nuclear weapons in foreign and defense policy, and the nature of the Western threat (including the character of relations with the United States)—highlights this trend.

■ The Role of Ideology in Foreign Policy

The boldest revision of foreign policy views to date has come with the leadership's determined effort to redefine the place of ideological considerations in the conceptualization and formulation of Soviet foreign policy. Indeed, as previously noted, Gorbachev has emphasized that he has striven to rid Soviet foreign policy of "ideological prejudices." These touch above all on the weight assigned to "class" factors as opposed to those of "state" interests in foreign affairs, thereby opening up a broad area for debate on the character of Soviet foreign-policy and security interests. While it is difficult to pinpoint the weight that this reexamination of the role of ideology has had in specific foreign-policy areas, there is hardly any area of Soviet foreign policy that would fail to be affected by it. The chief effect up to now has apparently been to throw open many previously settled issues, such as the character of peaceful coexistence, and thus of detente.

Gorbachev has repeatedly said that the emergence of "global" processes, including but not limited to nuclear weapons, has made it imperative for "class" values to be subordinate to "universal" values in the formulation of Soviet international policy. The stubborn reality of nuclear weapons, combined with the irreducible fact of economic and technological (as well as political?) interdependence, has as one crucial consequence advanced a redefinition of the Soviet concept of peaceful coexistence. During the Brezhnev period, peaceful coexistence was trumpeted consistently as an active form of the class struggle under conditions of nuclear deterrence. Indeed, all forms of intersystemic (i.e., capitalism versus socialism) struggle were to intensify under conditions of detente (defined as the process whereby the West was compelled by the USSR to accept peaceful coexistence as the *modus vivendi*), while inter-*state* relations were to be managed in such a way that the progressive triumph of socialism was safely secured. That, at least, was the theory, and while it would be wrong to apply such an obviously self-serving concept mechanically to Soviet policy of the period, there is no question but that such an aggressive view of detente informed both the tone and general direction of Soviet policy and came to cast a serious shadow over superpower relations. Oleg Bogomolov, Director of the Institute for the Study of the Economies of the World Socialist System, admits the validity of this perspective in his March 1988 open letter, in which he says that his institute, "in different notes and reports addressed to the highest authorities well before [the invasion of Afghanistan] in the middle of the 1970s, indicated that it was necessary to exercise restraint and caution in the turbulent area of the developing countries, so as not to threaten detente and the cause of disarmament."[72]

---

72. Oleg Bogomolov, "Kto zhe oshibalsya?" [Who Was Wrong?], *Literaturnaya Gazeta*, No. 11 (March 17, 1988), p. 10.

Now, Gorbachev, and his comrades, have formally rejected such a concept of peaceful coexistence. Gorbachev, Shevardnadze and, among the theorists, Primakov, have forcefully argued that peaceful coexistence can no longer be viewed as simply a "breathing spell" in the international class struggle, that it has become a more or less permanent *condition* of international life in the age of deterrence *cum* interdependence, and that the communists must adjust accordingly. In the process they have opened the prospect for the kind of East-West detente, based on pragmatic geopolitical considerations, that was theoretically excluded by the Brezhnevian concept of peaceful coexistence.[73]

In other areas as well, the Gorbachev leadership has challenged long-standing Soviet dogma, especially regarding the nature of "imperialism." In the series of questions he raised at the seventieth anniversary speech of November 2, 1987, and repeated at the ideological plenum in February 1988,[74] the general secretary has prepared the ground for a quantum leap in the way the USSR may perceive the international political environment facing it. By raising the possibility that imperialism may not require militarism, neocolonialism, and war, Gorbachev is implying (as had Varga in the 1940s and 1950s and Burlatsky in the 1970s)[75] that the fundamental *nature* (and not simply the conduct) of imperialism may be changing. If imperialism can be restrained not merely by the incessant application of Soviet power but by processes internal to imperialism (see pp. 48–51 on the nature of the threat), then the requirements for Soviet foreign and defense policy will have been significantly diminished. The attractiveness of such an argument for a politician with the kind of internal challenges that Gorbachev faces is apparent. Once again, the essential tie between internal Soviet priorities and foreign policy prevails.

■ *The Place of Nuclear Weapons in Foreign and Defense Policy*

The internal Soviet discussion on the impact of nuclear weapons on foreign and defense policy has also advanced markedly from the Brezhnev period. While such key

---

73. See Ligachev, *Pravda*, August 6, 1988, p. 2, for the contrasting view.
74. Gorbachev, "October and Perestroika," pp. 54–56.
75. See Lynch, *The Soviet Study of International Relations*, p. 114 and *passim*.

developments as the official recognition of nuclear stalemate—
on both the political and military-operational levels—find
their origins in the Brezhnev period (and even earlier), the
discussion of nuclear policy stopped at the point of parity
(conceived in numerical terms) with the Americans. Everything would be done to maintain parity, which was a signal
historical accomplishment of socialism, while the maintenance
of such parity was sufficient for security. Now that has
changed. Gorbachev provided the signal for this change with
his remark at the 27th Party Congress that, under contemporary conditions of an unregulated arms competition, parity
may no longer suffice to insure stable deterrence. Civilian
specialists within the foreign affairs research institutes, many
of whom had been occupying themselves with such problems
since the late 1970s, have been quick to advance the debate
from there.

In a series of journal articles published in the latter half of
1987, a number of political-military analysts developed the
concept of "reasonable sufficiency," and applied it to the
East-West arms relationship.[76] Parity, they write, is not a simple
quantitative concept. What counts is the ability of the USSR to
deliver a devastating counterblow, not the precise numerical
balance or the parallel development of weapons systems on
both sides. The realities of the nuclear balance are such that
deterrence is very stable within a broad range of weapons
balances. The criterion in Soviet nuclear weapons procurement
should be the capacity to maintain a reliable retaliatory force,
not what the Americans have *per se*. In the process, the authors
are evidently seeking to lay down new criteria for Soviet
military and arms control policy which, by establishing *mini-
mum* standards for credible deterrence, would help to demili-
tarize Soviet thinking about security and in the long run
release considerable resources now tied up in defense for
domestic economic and social development.

That these views are not merely voices in the wilderness is
shown by the vigorous reaction by the Soviet military during

76. In addition to Zhurkin *et al.*, see Zhurkin, "O razumnoy dostatochnosti"
(On Reasonable Sufficiency), *S.Sh.A.*, No. 12 (December 1987), pp. 11–21;
and Igor Malashenko, "Parity Reassessed," *New Times*, No. 47 (1987), pp.
9–10, and Malashenko, "Reasonable Sufficiency and Illusory Superiority," *New Times*, No. 24 (1987), pp. 18–20.

the second half of 1987 to much of the civilian discussion of nuclear weapons and policy, which by then had gone beyond the bounds of specialist discussion and had come to absorb the attention of the highly visible Writers Union.[77] When the rhetoric is separated from the analysis, what appears to concern the military is not the specific interpretation of deterrence offered by the civilian specialists but rather its public articulation, which they fear will have the effect of discrediting their mission within the armed forces and ultimately undermine their socializing role in Soviet society. (Could it be that this is exactly what Gorbachev, surveying the military stranglehold over much of Soviet culture, has in mind?)

A related point, brought to the fore by the American SDI program, concerns the future stability of the superpower arms balance. If even the maintenance of parity may not ensure stable deterrence, due to the pace of military-technological development and of possible qualitative leaps in the balance, and if superiority is not an attainable objective, then more effort must be devoted to restraining the military competition. A revised view of military sufficiency, as indicated above, would provide the USSR with greater flexibility in pursuing arms control options to institutionalize constraints on (primarily U.S.) military-technological development and its translation into fielded weapons systems. The *volte-face* in the Soviet position on the INF issue may only be the first shot in a series of such efforts to provide a more predictable, less threatening, and ultimately less costly strategic environment. While the outcome is not clear, an important debate with serious consequences for key institutional actors has been launched. In that process, concepts are evidently seen as deeds too.

---

77. See Thomas Nichols, "Intellectual Pacifists Criticized by Military Officer," *Radio Liberty Research*, RL 308–87, July 28, 1987; Nichols, "The Military and 'The New Political Thinking': Lizichev on Leninism and Defense," *Radio Liberty Research*, RL 80/87, February 26, 1987; Eugene Rumer, "Soviet Writers Clash Over Morality of Nuclear Deterrence," *Radio Liberty Research*, RL 299/87, July 13, 1987; Dominique Dhombres, "Le general et les pacifistes vegetariens," *Le Monde*, May 10–11, 1987, p. 5; and D. Volkogonov, "The Most Just War," *Kommunist*, No. 9 (June 1986), pp. 114–123 (JPRS translation UKO-86-016, October 21, 1986, pp. 130–140). For background, see F. Stephen Larrabee, "Gorbachev and the Soviet Military," *Foreign Affairs* (Summer 1988), pp. 1002-1026.

■ *The Character of the Western Threat*

In addition to these basic aspects of foreign and security policy, Gorbachev has made explicit revised views of the prospects for Western capitalism and for the political-military cohesion of the Western alliance, which bear strongly on how the Soviet leadership perceives the international environment facing it. As the new 1986 Soviet Party Program states, "Present-day capitalism differs in many respects from what it was . . . even in the middle of the twentieth century."[78] Gorbachev himself has said that "the present stage of the crisis [of capitalism] does not lead to any absolute stagnation of capitalism and does not rule out possible growth of its economy and the mastery of new scientific and technical trends." Most striking, Gorbachev observed at the Congress that the situation "allows for sustaining concrete economic, military, political, and other positions and in some cases even for possible social revenge, the regaining of what had been lost before."[79] This concern about a scientifically and economically recharged capitalist world contrasts sharply with the optimism of the 1970s, when the "correlation of forces" was said to be shifting constantly in favor of socialism.

As for Gorbachev's specific views on the cohesion of the Western alliance, he has acknowledged the strong ties that bind the United States and Western Europe. While fully admitting tendencies toward divergence on some political-military issues within the alliance framework, Gorbachev has declared himself a pragmatist on the issue of basic alliance unity. "The existing complex of economic, political-military and other common interests of the three centers of power [i.e., the United States, Western Europe and Japan]," Gorbachev told the Congress, "can hardly be expected to break up in the . . . present-day world."[80]

In addition, by late 1987 Gorbachev had begun to challenge basic ideological tenets concerning the character of imperialism and its proclivity to threaten international justice and stability. In so doing, Gorbachev has opened the door to a fuller discussion of an issue which, by touching on the nature

78. *Pravda,* March 7, 1986, p. 3, as translated in FBIS, *Daily Report-Soviet Union. (Supplement),* March 10, 1986, p. 1.
79. *Pravda,* February 26, 1986, p. 3 as translated in FBIS, *Daily Report-Soviet Union. (Supplement),* February 26, 1986, p. 5.
80. Ibid.

of the long-term international environment facing the USSR, has fundamental implications for Gorbachev's own intentions and flexibility in both foreign and domestic policies. The first public attempt to provide substance to this challenge appeared in *Kommunist*, the CPSU's theoretical journal, in early 1988.[81] In the article, three specialists issued a serious challenge to Soviet ideological orthodoxy on the nature of imperialism. In brief, the three argued that the combined effect of the existential deterrence exerted by nuclear weapons and deeply rooted democratic tendencies within Western societies had come to place strict limits on the ability of the imperialist West to threaten vital Soviet interests. Indeed, the authors write that the West is not interested in launching an aggressive war, "or any other war for that matter." They imply that the experience of June 22, 1941, i.e., the Nazi "surprise" attack, is no longer central to the contemporary Soviet Union. In its entirety the article ties together the discounting of the external threat, the requirements of sufficiency, and the general reorientation of Soviet policies toward domestic economic development. Certain to provoke widespread controversy within the Soviet Union, the article signals a further effort on the part of the leadership to redefine the external environment facing the USSR and thus control the political environment within the USSR.

One still looks, however, for analytically persuasive signs of Soviet admission of mutual responsibility for the collapse of detente. While many of the conceptual and doctrinal developments outlined above would seem to facilitate a more nuanced Soviet recognition of *mutual* responsibility for superpower relations, there has not yet been a systematic Soviet analysis of superpower ties that views them as a dynamic rather than unilateral phenomenon. Typical of much Soviet "analysis" is the following statement from one of the most sophisticated observers of Soviet-American relations, made in 1987: "The USSR has never had to introduce any changes in its policy [towards the U.S.] inasmuch as it has consistently directed its energies toward the improvement of Soviet-American relations, of the international situation as a whole."[82] As V. I.

---

81. See Zhurkin *et al.*, *Vyzovy bezopasnosti*.
82. Podlesnyi, "Razvitiye sovetsko-amerikanskikh otnosheniy v pervoy polovine 70-kh godov" [The Development of Soviet-American Relations in the First Half of the 1970s], in Trofimenko and Podlesnyi, eds., *Sovetsko-amerikanskiye otnosheniya*, p. 88.

Dashichev, the leading Soviet "revisionist" on foreign policy, recently said, "It was not the done thing in our country to talk about mistakes committed in our foreign policy. To this day, you will not find any mention at all in any book of a blunder or incorrect action."[83]

Recently, however, there is evidence that Soviet observers are beginning to examine U.S.-Soviet relations in a more complex way. On the policy level, Gorbachev speaks of the centrality of considering *mutual* interests in forging any stable superpower understanding, and implies that this embraces the ideological sphere and conflict in the Third World as well as bilateral state-to-state relations (which had been admitted by Brezhnev). On the specialist level, Soviet analysts have begun to speak of "the 'reverse' influence of the system of international relations upon the development of Soviet-American relations," of the impact of instability in the Third World (and thus superpower intervention) upon superpower relations ("the 'reverse' impact of regional problems on the general character of Soviet-American relations"), and of the proper nature and role of peaceful coexistence and "vital national interests" in superpower relations.[84] Even the link between the Stalinist system at home and Soviet foreign policy has been forcefully made, while specialists and even officials concede in general terms that the USSR made errors which formed part of the context of the collapse of detente (usually cited are the decision to deploy the SS-20 missile and the invasion of Afghanistan, safe topics now that the government has resolved each issue on the diplomatic level).[85] Raising such points,

---

83. *Komsomolskaya Pravda*, June 19, 1988, p. 3, as translated in *FBIS-SU*, June 20, 1988, p. 56.
84. Podlesnyi, "Razvitiye sovetsko-amerikanskikh otnosheniy," pp. 5–10.
85. As per Bogomolov, "Kto zhe oshibal'sya?" V. I. Dashichev, in a remarkable article in *Literaturnaya Gazeta*, May 18, 1988, p. 14, argued that the nature of the Stalinist system made "understandable" Western reservations about cooperating with the USSR in the late 1930s and after World War II. For examples of this new tendency towards self-criticism in foreign policy, see Shevardnadze's speech to the UN, *Izvestiya*, June 10, 1988, p. 4, where he ties Soviet foreign policy to a "self-critical reevaluation of our own past and the mistakes that were committed"; V. Israelyan (senior career diplomat), "Mir ne mozhet byt' zaklyuchen tol'ko sverkhu" [Peace Can't Be Achieved Only From Above], *Literaturnaya Gazeta*, June 15, 1988, p. 14; A. Bovin, "Perestroika i vneshnyaya politika" [Reform and Foreign Policy], *Izvestiya*, June 16, 1988, p. 5; "Past Foreign Policy 'Blunders' Criticized," *FBIS-SU*, June 20, 1988, pp. 56–58 (from

however, constitutes only a start to any realistic Soviet analysis of superpower relations. Yet many of the constituent elements for such an analysis have already been laid down elsewhere, as we have seen, suggesting that quite a vigorous discussion has been going on behind closed doors. Given the sensitivity of the subject to any Soviet leader, perhaps this discussion can only take place in indirect form. One should not expect Soviet observers to flay themselves for undermining detente in the 1970s; but further development of a more visible reassurance to Western interlocutors that the Soviets now accept their share of the blame and are prepared to act accordingly would be a significant sign of change.

Komsomol'skaya Pravda, June 19, 1988, p. 3); remarks at news conference by First Deputy Foreign Minister Yuli Vorontsov and Chief of General Staff Marshal Sergei Akhromeev, The Financial Times, June 27, 1988, p. 2; "Roundtable on Past, Present Foreign Policy," FBIS-SU, June 30, 1988, pp. 4–9 (from Literaturnaya Gazeta, June 29, 1988, p. 14); Foreign Minister Shevardnadze's speech to Foreign Ministry personnel, Pravda, July 26, 1988, p. 4; and the TASS report of the Foreign Ministry conference, Pravda, July 28, 1988, p. 4. For a contrary view, which should be seen in light of Ligachev's foreign policy dissent in Gorky on August 5, see the article by Valentin Falin and Lev Bezymensky blaming the U.S. for the Cold War, Pravda, August 29, 1988, p. 6 (translated in FBIS-SU, August 31, 1988, p. 6–11).

6

Actors and Analysts: Supporters of the "New Thinking"

How broadly shared among Gorbachev's political colleagues is the "new thinking" that has come to symbolize Gorbachev's approach to foreign policy? In fact, the dedicated exponents of the new *thinking*, as opposed to just new language, appear to be limited to a very few politicians and advisors, judging by the analytical rather than the rhetorical content of what the Soviet leadership has been saying. Significantly, however, some of the most forceful supporters of the "new thinking" occupy positions of great authority within the leadership, while others have been steadily promoted to important advisory positions.

As we have seen, Foreign Minister Shevardnadze is a key exponent of the new Soviet approach to foreign affairs. In two remarkable speeches to the diplomatic and foreign affairs corps in June/July 1987, Shevardnadze laid absolute priority upon domestic economic development in the formulation and conduct of foreign policy and severely criticized past Soviet foreign policy for inflexibility and unrealistic objectives.[86] In the latter speech Shevardnadze made a strong plea for the priority of "common sense" over ideology in foreign affairs. An effective politician who evidently, like Gorbachev, thinks for himself and has come to be much more than caretaker of the Foreign Ministry, Shevardnadze serves to insure that the priorities of the leadership are now strictly reflected in the ministry's standard operating procedures and its role in foreign and security policy.

---

86. *Vestnik MID SSSR*, No. 2 (1987), pp. 30–34; and "Shevardnadze on Decentralizing Economic Ties," FBIS, *Soviet Union-Daily Report*, October 30, 1987, pp. 49–53.

Politburo member Aleksandr N. Yakovlev, now party secretary responsible for international affairs and the daily moving force behind the *glasnost'* campaign, also figures as a key supporter of the "new thinking" and as a critical link between the analytical community and the political leadership. As a career politician who uniquely (through a ten-year ambassadorship in Canada and brief tenure as head of IMEMO) bestrides both domestic and foreign policy, it is difficult to overestimate the significance of Yakovlev's position in the top leadership. Ironically, it is difficult, if not impossible, to derive Yakovlev's role in the "new thinking" from much of his published writing on international relations, especially when it concerns the United States. When he writes about "inter-imperialist relations" and U.S.-West European alliance dynamics, however, Yakovlev proves himself to be a much more sophisticated and nuanced observer.[87] His name is always mentioned inside the USSR as one of the key movers behind the "new thinking" campaign, and there is indirect proof—in the form of a most unorthodox article on Soviet foreign policy in the January 1988 edition of *Kommunist*—to suggest that Yakovlev has indeed lent his considerable political weight to the promotion of new ideas, and people, in order to advance the discussion on Soviet foreign-policy priorities in the years ahead.[88] Politburo member Vadim Medvedev, now party secretary for ideological affairs and a strong exponent of the primacy of "general human" values over class values in foreign policy, may also be added to this list.

Other key players in pushing for "new thinking" include Gorbachev's advisor Georgi Shakhnazarov, who is also President of the Soviet Political Science Association and has played

---

87. Compare his "Peace American Style and Modern Realities," in *Peace & Disarmament. Academic Studies* (Moscow: Progress, 1985), pp. 173–189, with his interview with *La Repubblica* and "Imperializm: sopernichestvo i protivorechiya" [Imperialism: Competition and Contradictions], *Pravda*, March 23, 1984, pp. 3–4.
88. V. Zhurkin, S. Karaganov, A. Kortunov, "Vyzovy bezopasnosti—starye i novye" [The Challenges of Security—Old and New], *Kommunist*, No. 1 (1988), pp. 42–50. The argument runs parallel to a key ideological speech by Yakovlev arguing that the military competition is a trap laid by the West to exhaust the USSR economically and that consequently the USSR should refuse to play tit-for-tat in that sphere, concentrating instead on its economic, social, political and ideological development. See *Vestnik Akademii Nauk*, No. 6 (1987).

a key role in advancing the Soviet study of international relations in the past decade and a half. Shakhnazarov's writings, going back to the mid-1970s, show him to be the advocate of a very pragmatic, "power-realist" analysis of international relations, arguing that national "patriotism" rather than "internationalism" will remain the mainspring of world politics for the foreseeable future. He is also the author of a remarkable quote from the early 1980s: "While the correlation of forces constantly changes in favor of socialism, that does not mean any specific superiority of socialism over capitalism."[89]

One may also cite Vladimir Petrovsky, Deputy Minister of Foreign Affairs and for many years a specialist on international-relations theory and especially U.S. foreign-policy doctrines.[90] Petrovsky (among others) has been heard to quote Hans Morgenthau fondly in attempting to encapsulate the essence of the current Soviet foreign-policy approach, and in this sense his power-oriented pragmatism unites him with Shakhnazarov. Petrovsky is reported to have drafted Gorbachev's September 17, 1987, *Pravda* article calling for a new approach to the United Nations and to multilateral institutions more generally, and is clearly a key governmental link in the translation of new policy concepts into practicable policy choices and proposals.

Finally, we may add Yevgeny Primakov, Director of IMEMO and designated head of the new Academy of Sciences Department for World Economy and International Relations; Aleksandr Bovin of *Izvestiya* and Fyodor Burlatsky of *Literaturnaya Gazeta* in the press; and within the research institutes Vitaly Zhurkin, Director of the new Institute of Europe; and Andrei Kokoshin, heir apparent to Georgy Arbatov in the Institute of U.S. and Canada Studies. In sum, it would appear that personal links are key to the promulgation of the "new thinking" both among the leadership and between the analytical community and the top leadership. Much of the dynamics of this process thus remains hidden from view. Yet indisputably, Mikhail Gorbachev has set about to put in place a team of

---

89. For a list of Shakhnazarov's pertinent writings, see Lynch, *The Soviet Study of International Relations* pp. 189–190.
90. See his *Amerikanskaya vneshne-politicheskaya mysl'* [U.S. Foreign Policy Thought] (Moscow: Mezhdunarodnye Otnosheniya, 1976). For other works, see Lynch, *The Soviet Study of International Relations*, p. 187.

political colleagues, governmental specialists, and academic advisers that can serve as the core of the "new thinking" in, to paraphrase Clausewitz, a very resistant medium.[91]

■ *How Has the Role of Foreign-Policy Specialists Changed?*

To the extent that Soviet foreign-policy specialists have found their role in the policy-making process changing recently, it is first of all because the general political climate within the country has changed. Certainly, their ideas, however persuasive, were not so powerful as to change the intellectual receptivity of the Soviet leadership by themselves. What appears to have happened is that, based on the impact of the external and internal factors discussed in pages 39–42, Gorbachev and his colleagues have encouraged—through exhortation, recruitment and display of a new receptivity—the development of a more open internal discussion of foreign-policy problems that could provide the leadership with the kind of reliable information and fresh ideas that it has determinedly sought in the domestic economic sphere. This apparently includes the encouragement of unorthodox civilian analysis to provoke responses by the military, so as to make military-operational assumptions open and provide important information to the leadership. This has been reinforced by Gorbachev's general opening to Soviet intellectuals, as he seeks to construct his own rather unorthodox power base.

Personal ties, as in any political system, appear to have played a decisive role in advancing "new thinking," and new thinkers, in the age of Gorbachev. Curiously, the originators of the term, Anatoly Gromyko and Lev Lomeiko (in their 1984 book *New Thinking in the Nuclear Age*),[92] do not seem to have had a significant follow-up role in the elaboration of Gorbachev's revised foreign-policy vision. We have already mentioned, besides Gorbachev and Shevardnadze, the important part that Aleksandr Yakovlev, Georgy Shakhnazarov, Vladimir Pe-

---

91. Evidence that the "new political thinking" is taking root is provided by the first public reaction against it by Yegor Ligachev, *Pravda*, August 6, 1988, p. 2. The issue has thus been joined; how it is resolved will say much about the future policy impact of the new political thinking as indeed of the reform policy as a whole. *Pravda*, August 6, 1988, p. 2, as translated in *FBIS-SU*, August 8, 1988, p. 39.
92. See footnote 41.

trovsky and Yevgeny Primakov have played in this respect. We should perhaps also add Roald Sagdeyev, Director of the Institute for Space Research, for his contribution to revising the Soviet estimate (downward) of the threat posed by SDI as well as for his work, in collaboration with social scientists from the research institutes, on problems of strategic stability. All have assisted in the promotion, execution and dissemination of research and analysis elaborating on aspects of the "new political thinking" and securing it greater political visibility.

Because political changes, which are still unfolding, lie behind the newfound prominence accorded to the view of many old new-thinkers, it is too early to pronounce definitively upon the nature of the specialists' relationship to policy. However, a number of recent institutional changes suggest that the political leadership is trying to integrate foreign-policy research work more effectively into the conceptualization and formulation of foreign policy. Within the Foreign Ministry, a new bureau for research has been established, headed by senior Ambassador Vladimir Shustov, long involved in Soviet-American affairs and reputed to be one of the movers behind the revised Soviet attitude to international organizations. In staffing the bureau, Shustov has brought in research scholars from outside institutes, including political-military analysts from the Institute of U.S. and Canada Studies. Deputy Foreign Minister Petrovsky's long-standing interest in international-relations research, especially on issues relating to U.S. policy, disarmament and the United Nations, suggest some of the directions for the Foreign Ministry's operational research.

On March 17, 1988, the Soviet Academy of Sciences decided upon a reorganization of the Academy's international-relations research institutes. Effective January 1, 1989, all foreign-policy institutes were removed from under the wing of the Economics Division (headed by Abel Aganbegyan) to a new division entitled "World Economy and International Relations," headed by IMEMO Director Yevgeny Primakov. By thus clarifying lines of communication, Primakov may be able to effect a more productive integration of research, policy analysis and policy. He, and his colleagues in the institutes, will also certainly try to clarify the academic standing of their institutions and research agendas with the Academy. At the moment, much of their more innovative work falls between the cracks of the traditional scientific disciplines established by the Academy and the ideological ones presided over by the adherents of "scientific communism." (As one Soviet expert put it, "Where do you fit a dissertation on the 'Psychology of Deterrence'?") Their ability to do so will largely depend on how they manage their own in-house affairs: whether the U.S. and Canada Institute, for example, can de-bureaucratize itself from managing its international contacts and organizational work to do more fundamental, innovative background research to fill in such concepts as "reasonable sufficiency" and "non-provocative defense." It will also depend, of course, on the evolution of the domestic political situation.

Interestingly, there may be a special role to be assigned to the newly established Institute of Europe. The purview of the Institute plus its staffing—its Director is Vitaly Zhurkin with a senior staff including Sergei Karaganov, both authors of the controversial January 1988 *Kommunist* article—strongly suggest the guiding hand of Politburo member Aleksandr Yakovlev. Conceivably, this could become the " 'new thinking' Institute," with a direct channel to the top via Yakovlev, to provide the leadership with the kind of alternative operational research support that is currently not available and which it may not be capable of getting in a timely way from existing institutions. Whatever its exact role, there can be little doubt that the establishment of this institute is part and parcel of the process whereby, as Primakov said in a keynote article on Soviet international-relations research, "the tasks assigned by the 27th Party Congress for the activization of the social sciences . . . [stimulate] both the theoretical development and the implementation of the practical activity of the CPSU and the Soviet state."[93]

---

93. Yevgeny Primakov, "XXVII s"ezd KPSS i issledovaniye problem mirovoy ekonomiki i mezhdunarodnykh otnosheniy" [The 27th CPSU Party Congress and Research on Problems of World Economy and International Relations], *Mirovaya Ekonomika i Mezhdunarodnye Otnosheniya*, No. 6 (1986), p. 14.

7

Conclusion

The emerging contemporary Soviet view of international relations reviewed in this paper, in contrast to the traditional Leninist/Stalinist conception, stresses the (relative) independence of political activity from "objective" socioeconomic factors; the primacy of the state over classes in international politics; and the potentially decisive impact of the international system, characterized by increasing multipolarity and diversity of national interests, upon the policies of its constituent states. Given this analytical framework, Soviet observers can no longer claim to deduce international political behavior primarily from the "class character" (capitalist or socialist) of specific states or group of states. Consequently, international relations—seen as essentially interstate relations—must be analyzed in their own terms and no longer as a subordinate branch of political economy. Drawing a qualitative distinction between internal politics (where class struggle prevails) and international politics (where class compromise follows from the power structure of international relationships), Soviet analysts and the general secretary himself display an increasing grasp of the indeterminate, political quality of world politics. Taking into account the recognition that nuclear war can be neither an instrument nor a continuation of policy, and the consequent redefinition of "peaceful coexistence" from a tool of the global class struggle to a condition for mutual survival, Soviet politicians and policy intellectuals have effected a virtual turnabout in the traditional Soviet concept of international relations.

This increasingly sophisticated and pragmatic approach serves as the intellectual background to Gorbachev's foreign-policy vision and predisposes Soviet international policy toward the achievement of more moderate and narrowly focused goals then has usually been ascribed to it. Because the international system, in its basic determinants, is *not* seen to be a revolutionary one, revolutionary objectives are not appropriate to the advancement of Soviet interests. The frustration of Soviet revolutionary aspirations, long ago in the West and now in much of the Third World as well, has forced a lowering of Soviet sights. Recognition of the universally fatal consequences of a collapse of the international order through global war has in turn provided the USSR with a convincing stake in the stability of that order, certainly for any policy-relevant future. In less dramatic manner, the complexities of international economic, ecological and intellectual interdependence have foreclosed autarky as a serious political alternative—the issue now revolves about the kind and scope of that interdependence, rather than its existence.

All of this has brought into sharp focus the importance of the international system for the USSR, and thus of the interaction of both internal and external factors in shaping the policy choices before the Soviet leadership. Gorbachev's injunction that Soviet foreign policy, and international stability, must be based on a full consideration of the "mutual interests" involved, thus deserves to be taken seriously. While these new perspectives do not in themselves lead to specific policy outcomes (nor could they, due to the *external* impulses affecting Soviet foreign policy-making), they do reflect a different sensibility in the formulation of foreign policy, one that is more international in outlook, more pragmatic in its basic expectations from policy, more conscious of the multiple hindrances to the easy extension of Soviet power and influence abroad, and potentially more responsive to constructive international initiatives than any in the Soviet past.

Because the new Soviet approach to foreign policy has been shaped in important measure as a reaction to external forces and circumstances, the precise content of both theory and practice will depend in part on the pattern of interaction between the Soviet Union and the international community, in the first place the Western political alliance, headed by the United States. It is thus within the power of the West, at the margins, to advance or retard the process of adaptation to prevailing international realities (and by extension the course of reform within the USSR) that characterized much policy analysis even under Brezhnev and that has now found expression in the strategy and tactics of Mikhail Gorbachev. Whether the West is capable of negotiating such a subtle engagement with the Soviet leadership remains to be seen. That will depend not simply on the West's Soviet policies, of exploiting the opportunities presented by the new turn in Soviet foreign policy, but on its ability to manage the international political economy and its own alliance system.

Viewed historically, contemporary Soviet attitudes toward foreign affairs may be interpreted as confirmation of a Western policy of containment combining military strength and political flexibility toward the goal of encouraging a more realistic adaptation by the Soviet leadership to its international environment. Ironically, many of the contemporary Soviet statements on "mutual security," "interdependence," "global problems," and the intractability of Third World development, echo prevailing Western views of the early 1970s. In response to a series of aggressive projections of political-military power by the USSR in the mid- to late-1970s, culminating in the invasion of Afghanistan, the West, and especially the United States, quickly shed this rhetoric in favor of more unilateral approaches to security, which in a sense mirrored official Soviet views at that time. In certain ways, the West remains transfixed by the image of Soviet power that developed during the late 1970s, while the Soviets themselves are adopting approaches comparable to those widespread in the West in the early 1970s.[94] If this cycle is not to continue, with each side reacting to the frustration of its purposes by adopting an increasingly unilateral approach to security, both must adapt creatively to the break that the Gorbachev leadership is making with important aspects of the Soviet past. For that to happen, all parties involved will have to do some thinking anew. As a first step, it would be useful if each side began to pay closer attention to how the other has been thinking about the character of their interrelationship.

---

94. See Zdenek Mlynar, "Neue Ideen in der sowjetischen Aussenpolitik," *Mediatus*, No. 3 (1987), pp. 3–7. For a fuller statement of Mlynar's views, see his forthcoming book, *Was Kann Gorbatschow Andern? Politische Reform in der UdSSR und ihre internationale Aspekte* (Laxenburg, Austria: August 1988), pp. 170–206 (manuscript form).

Appendix
Excerpts, Speech by Mikhail Gorbachev, "October and Revolution: The Revolution Continues," November 2, 1987

Translation provided by the Mission of the USSR to the United Nations.

. . . During the few years when Lenin directed Soviet foreign policy, he not only worked out its underlying principles but also showed how they should be applied in the most unusual and abruptly changing situations.

Indeed, contrary to initial expectations, the rupture of the "weakest link" in the chain of the capitalist system was not the "last, decisive battle" but the beginning of a long and complex process.

It was a major achievement of the founder of the Soviet State that he discerned in time the actual prospects the victory in the Civil War opened before the new Russia.

He realized that the country had secured not merely a "breathing spell" but something much more important—"a new period, in which we have won the right to our fundamental international existence in the network of capitalist states". In a resolute step, Lenin suggested a policy of learning and mastering the art of long-term "existence side by side" with them. Countering leftist extremism, he argued that it was possible for countries with different social systems to coexist peacefully.

It took only 18 to 24 months in the wake of the Civil War to end the international political isolation of the state of workers and peasants.

Treaties were concluded with neighboring countries and then, at Rapallo, with Germany. Britain, France, Italy, Sweden and other capitalist countries extended diplomatic recognition to the Soviet Republic.

The first steps were taken to build equitable relations with oriental countries—China, Turkey, Iran and Afghanistan.

These were not simply the first victories of Lenin's foreign policy and diplomacy. They were a breakthrough into a fundamentally new quality of international affairs.

The main thrust of our foreign policy has remained unchanged. We have every right to describe it as a Leninist policy of peace, mutually beneficial international cooperation and friendship among nations.

Naturally, not all our subsequent foreign policy efforts were successful. We have had our share of setbacks. We did not make full use of all the opportunities that opened before us both before and after World War Two.

We failed to translate the enormous moral prestige with which the Soviet Union emerged from the war into effective efforts to consolidate the peaceloving, democratic forces and to stop those who orchestrated the Cold War. We did not always respond adequately to imperialist provocations.

It is true that some things could have been tackled better and that we could have been more efficient. Nevertheless, we can say on this memorable occasion that the overall thrust of our policy has remained in concert with the basic course worked out and charted by Lenin—consonant with the very nature of socialism, with its principled commitment to peace.

This was overwhelmingly instrumental in averting the outbreak of a nuclear war and in preventing imperialism from winning the Cold War.

Together with our allies, we defeated the imperialist strategy of "rolling back socialism". Imperialism had to curb its claims to world domination. The results of our peaceloving policy were what we could draw on at the new stage to devise fresh approaches in the spirit of the new political thinking.

Naturally, there have been changes in the Leninist concept of peaceful coexistence. At first it was needed above all to create a modicum of external conditions for the construction of a new society in the country of the Socialist Revolution.

Continuing the class-based policy of the victorious proletariat, peaceful coexistence later, particularly in the nuclear age, become a condition for the survival of the entire human race.

The April 1985 Plenary Meeting of the CPSU Central Committee was a landmark in the development of Leninist thought along this line too. The new concept of foreign policy was presented in detail at the 27th Congress.

As you know, this concept proceeds from the idea that for all the profound contradictions of the contemporary world, for all the radical differences among the countries that comprise it, it is interrelated, interdependent and integral.

The reasons for this include the internationalization of world economic ties, the comprehensive scope of the scientific and technological revolution, the essentially novel role played by the mass media, the state of the earth's resources, the common environmental danger, and the crying social problems of the developing world which affect us all.

This problem is now with us because the development of nuclear weapons and the threatening prospect of their use have called into question the very survival of the human race.

That was how Lenin's idea about the priority of the interests of social development acquired a new meaning and a new importance. The main reason, however, is the problem of human survival.

What, then are the reasons for our optimism, for regarding comprehensive security really attainable: This deserves to be discussed here in detail.

At this new turning point in world history as we celebrate the 70th anniversary of our Revolution which could not have won without theoretical preparation, we are examining the theoretical aspects of the prospects of advancement to durable peace.

The new way of thinking has helped us to generally prove that a comprehensive system of international security in the context of disarmament is needed and possible.

Now we must prove that the attainment of this goal is necessary and feasible. We must identify the laws governing the interaction of the forces which, through rivalry, contradictions and conflicting interest, can produce the desired effect.

In this connection we should begin by posing some tough questions—of course, tackling them from Leninist positions and using Leninist methodology.

The first question relates to the nature of imperialism. We know that it is the major source of the war threat.

It goes without saying that external factors cannot change the nature of a social system. But, given the current stage of the world's development and the new level of its interdependence and integration, is it possible to influence that nature and block its more dangerous manifestations?

In other words, can one count on the laws operating in the integral world, in which universal human values have top priority, to restrict the scope of the destructive effects produced by the operation of the egocentric laws which benefit only the ruling classes and are basic to the capitalist system?

The second question is connected with the first one: can capitalism get rid of militarism and function and develop in the economic sphere without it? Is it not a delusion on our part to invite the West to draw up and compare conversion programmes for switching the economy to civilian production?

The third question: can the capitalist system do without neocolonialism which is currently one of the factors essential to its survival?

In other words, can this system function without the practices of inequitable trade with the third world, fraught with unforeseeable consequences?

Another related question: how realistic is our hope that the awareness of the terrible threat the world is facing—and we know that this awareness is making its way even into the higher echelons of the Western ruling elite—will be translated into practical policies?

After all, however forceful the arguments of common sense, however well-developed the sense of responsibility, however powerful the instinct of self-preservation, there are still things which must not be underrated and which are determined by an economic and, consequently, a class-based self-interest.

In other words, the question is whether capitalism can adapt itself to the conditions of a new and equitable economic order, to the conditions in which the intellectual and moral values of the two world systems will be compared honestly. These are far from idle questions. The course history will take in the coming decades will depend on the way they are answered.

But even posing these questions is enough to grasp the gravity of the task that lies ahead. We will see them answered in due time. Meanwhile, the viability of the programme for a nuclear-free and safe world will not only depend on its flawless scientific substantiation but will also be tested by the course of events—something that is influenced by a wide variety of factors, many of them new.

It is in fact already being tested. Here, too, we are loyal to the Leninist tradition, to the very essence of Leninism—an organic blend of theory and practice, an approach to theory as a tool of practice as a mechanism verifying the viability of theory.

That is how we are acting, projecting the new way of thinking onto our foreign policy activities, adjusting and specifying it by political experience.

To sum up, what do we count on in our awareness that a safe world will have to be built jointly with capitalist countries?

The postwar period has witnessed an in-depth modification of the contradictions that used to determine the principal trends in the world's economy and politics. I refer above all to the trends that inevitably led to wars, to world wars between capitalist countries themselves.

Today the situation is different. It is not only the lessons of the past war but also the fear of sapping its own strength in the face of socialism, by now a world system, that have prevented capitalism from allowing its "internal" contradictions to go to extremes.

These contradictions began to evolve into a technological race against competitors and were dampened with the help of neo-colonialism. A kind of latter-day "peaceful" repartitioning of the world was started, in line with the rule Lenin identified—"according to capital", the bigger share going to whoever was strongest and wealthiest at the moment.

Some countries began to "ease" tensions in their economies by rechannelling resources into the military-industrial complex on the pretext of a "Soviet threat". The changes occurring within the technological and organizational infrastructure of the capitalist economy also helped to allay contradictions and to balance different interests.

But that is not all there is to it. Since an alliance between a socialist country and capitalist states proved possible in the past, when the threat of Fascism arose, does this not suggest a lesson for the present, for today's world which faces the threat of nuclear catastrophe and the need to ensure safe nuclear power production and overcome the danger to environment?

These are all perfectly real and acute problems. Grasping them is not enough: practical solutions must also be found.

The next point. Can a capitalist economy develop without militarization? This brings to mind the "economic miracle" in Japan, West Germany and Italy—although it is true that when the "miracle" was over, they switched to militarism again.

But here one should examine the degree to which this switch was rooted in the substantive laws governing the operation of contemporary monopoly capital and the role played by extraneous factors—the "contagious example" of the U.S. military-industrial complex, the Cold War and its spirit, considerations of prestige, the desire to have one's own "mailed fist" to be able to talk to one's competitors in a commonly understood language, and the intention to back one's economic invasion of the third world with power politics.

Whatever the actual reasons, there was a period when the modern capitalist economy developed rapidly in several countries whose arms spending was minimal. The relevant historical experience is available.

This issue can also be considered from a different angle, the other way round.

Ever since the war, the U.S. economy has been oriented and dependent on militarism which at first seemed even to stimulate it. But then this senseless and socially useless squandering of resources led to an astronomical national debt and to other problems and maladies.

In the final analysis it has turned out that super-militarization increasingly aggravates the domestic situation and upsets the economies of other countries.

The recent panic on the New York stock exchange and on other stock exchanges across the world—a panic without precedent in almost 60 years—is a grave symptom and a grave warning.

The third point: the inequitable, exploitative relations with the developing countries. For all the fantastic innovations in the creation of an "alternative (man-made) environment", developed capitalism has been and will be unable to do without these countries' resources. That is an objective fact.

The calls for severing the historically shaped world economic ties are dangerous and offer no solution.

But the neocolonialist methods of using the resources of others, the arbitrary practices of the transnational corporations, the debt-related bondage, the debts that are nearing the trillion-dollar mark and obviously cannot be repaid, also lead to an impasse.

All this gives rise to acute problems within the capitalist countries themselves too. The various speculations on this score are essentially aimed at making the third world a kind of scapegoat and blaming it for the numerous difficulties—including the falling living standards—in the metropolitan countries, while making the masses accept the policy of latter-day capitalist modernization.

However, none of these or similar stratagems can do away with the problem itself. They can only mitigate it temporarily. Inequitable trade remains a fact that will eventually culminate in an explosion. It appears that Western leaders are beginning to understand that this outcome is a distinct possibility—but so far, they have been merely trying to resort to various stopgap measures.

Indeed, the novelty of the international economic and political processes of our time has not yet been fully grasped and assimilated.

Yet, this will have to be done because the ongoing processes have the force of an objective law: either a disaster or a joint quest for a new economic order taking into account the interests of all on an equal basis.

The way to establishing such an order, as we see it today, has become discernible: through implementing the "disarmament-for-development" concept.

Thus, when looking for an answer to our third question, too, we see that the situation does not seem to defy resolution. In this area as well contradictions can be modified. But this necessitates understanding reality and mapping out practical actions in the spirit of the new thinking.

And this, in turn, will facilitate the advance towards a more secure world. In a nutshell, here as well we are facing a historic choice dictated by the laws of our largely interconnected and integral world.

There is another important, even decisive, fact. Socialism is a component of this world. Having embarked on its history 70 years ago and then grown into a world system, it has in fact determined the character of the 20th century. Today it is entering a new stage in its development, demonstrating once again its inherent potentialities.

Think, for instance, of the vast potentialities for peaceful coexistence inherent in just the Soviet Union's perestroika.

By making it possible for us to attain the world level in all major economic indicators, perestroika will enable our vast and wealthy country to become involved in the world division of labor and resources in a way never known before.

Its great scientific, technological and production potential will become a far more substantial component of world economic relations.

This will decisively broaden and strengthen the material base of the all-embracing system of peace and international security. And that, by the way, is another highly important aspect of perestroika, the place it is assigned in contemporary civilization.

The class struggle and other manifestations of social contradictions will influence the objective processes favoring peace. The advanced forces of the working-class movement are looking for ways to raise its political awareness.

They have to carry on their activities in a highly complicated, new and changing situation. The questions of safeguarding the economic rights and interests of the masses, and indeed those related to the struggle for democracy, including democracy in production, have acquired a new meaning.

For instance, workers are sometimes offered a "partnership", but it is a partnership under which access to the sanctum of business is shut off for them and free election of the top-level managerial personnel is out of the question.

The Western world abounds in "theories" treating of the disappearance of the working class, and claiming that it has become completely dissolved in the "middle class", socially changed, and so on and so forth. True, the changes undergone by the working class are substantial and far-reaching. But it is to no purpose that its class adversary is seeking consolation in this and trying to disorient and confuse the working-class movement.

The working class, a numerically predominant force today within its new social boundaries, has the potential to play a decisive role, especially at abrupt turning points in history.

The motives for that may be different. One of the most probable ones is the insane militarization of the economy. The transition to a new phase of the technological revolution on militarist grounds may serve as a powerful catalyst, especially as it paves the way to war, thus affecting all sections of the population and taking mass protests beyond the limits of economic demands.

Therefore, here, too, the ruling class, the masters of monopoly capital, will have to make a choice. It is our belief, and it is confirmed by science, that at the present level of technology and organization of production, the reconversion and demilitarization of the economy are feasible. This would be tantamount to opting for peace.

The same concerns the consequences of the crisis in relations between the developed and the developing world.

If things come to the verge of an explosion and it proves no longer possible to enjoy the benefits of exploiting the third world, the unacceptable and inadmissible character of a system which cannot exist otherwise may acquire a political dimension, and very acutely at that.

In sum, in this sense, too, capitalism is facing a limited choice—either to let things reach the breaking point or to heed the laws of the interconnected and integral world, one that calls for a balance of interest on an equal basis.

The situation, as we see it, makes this not only necessary, but possible too. The more so as forces in the third world are acting along the same lines.

The decline of the national liberation movement is a common phrase. However, what apparently happens is that concepts are substituted and the novelty of the situation is ignored.

As far as the impulse for liberation is concerned, the one that was present at the stage of the struggle for political independence, it is certainly waning. And this is only natural.

As for the impulse essential to the new, current stage of the third world's development, it is only nascent. One has to be aware of this and refrain from yielding to pessimism. The factors that make up the impulse are varied and far from simple.

Among them is a powerful economic process which sometimes takes on paradoxical forms. For instance, certain countries, while retaining some features of backwardness, are attaining a great power level in the world economy and politics.

There is also a rise in political vigour as nations are formed and genuine nation-states, among which an important place is held by countries with revolutionary regimes.

There is also the wrath bred by the dramatic polarization of poverty and wealth, and the contrast between possibilities and realities.

An urge for national identity and initiative makes itself increasingly felt in the organizations reflecting the processes of inter-state consolidation among the developing countries.

To a greater or lesser extent this is characteristic of all the organizations, and their number is not small—the Organization of African Unity, the League of Arab States, the ASEAN, the Organization of American States, the Latin American Economic System, the South Pacific Forum, the South Asian Association for Regional Cooperation, the Organization of the Islamic Conference and, especially, the non-aligned movement.

They represent a wide spectrum of conflicting interests, needs, aspirations, ideologies, claims, and prejudices typical of precisely this stage. Although they have already turned into a noticeable factor in world politics, none of them has yet fully revealed its potentialities. But the potentialities are colossal, and it is even hard to predict what they will yield in the coming 50 years.

One thing is clear: this is a world of its own, seeking organizational forms for effective and equitable participation in solving problems common to the whole of humankind. It stands for two and a half billion people.

One can envision the gigantic strides it will make not only in exerting its influence on world politics, but also in playing an original role in shaping the world economy of the future.

For all their might, it is not the transnationals that will determine the third world's development; it is more likely that they will be forced to adjust to the independent choice that has been or will be made by the peoples.

The peoples and the organizations representing them have a stake in the new world economic order.

There is another important point to be made. In the last few decades, development within the capitalist world proper has given rise to new forms of social contradictions and movements.

Among them are movements to remove the nuclear threat, protect the environment, eliminate racial discrimination, rule out policies dividing society into the privileged and the underprivileged, prevent the disaster threatening industrial areas that have fallen victim to present-day capitalist modernization.

These movements involve millions of people and are inspired and led by prominent figures in science and culture, people enjoying national and international prestige.

Social democratic, socialist and labor parties and mass organizations similar to or connected with them continuously play an important role in the political processes in a number of countries, and the influence of some of them is increasing.

Thus, according to all economic, political and social indications everywhere in today's world the thesis Lenin regarded as one of the most profound in Marxism is being vindicated: as the thoroughness of the historical action grows, the mass whose action it is will grow as well.

And this is always an unmistakable sign and the most powerful factor of social progress and, consequently, of peace.

Indeed, the grandeur and novelty of our time is determined by the peoples' increasingly obvious and open presence in the foreground of history. Their present position is such that they must be heeded immediately rather than in the long run.

The new truth thereby brought into sharp focus is that a constant need to make a choice is increasingly characteristic of historical advancement as we are about to enter the 21st century. And the right choice depends on the extent to which the interests and aspirations of millions and hundreds of millions of people are heeded.

Hence the politicians' responsibility. For policy can only be effective if the novelty of the time is taken into account—today the human factor figures on the political plane not as a remote and more or less spontaneous side effect of the life, activity and intentions of the masses. It directly invades world affairs.

Unless this is realized, in other words, unless the new thinking, one based on current realities and the peoples' will, is adopted, politics turn into an unpredictable improvisation posing a risk both to one's own country and to other nations. Such politics have no lasting support.

Such are the reasons for our optimistic view of the future, of the prospects of creating an all-embracing system of international security.

This is the logic behind our stand on defence issues, too. As long as there is a danger of war and as long as the drive for social revanche forms the core of Western strategies and militarist programmes, we shall continue to do everything necessary to maintain our defense capability at a level ruling out imperialism's military superiority over socialism.

Comrades, during these jubilee days, we duly commend the accomplishments of the world communist movement.

The time of the Communist International, the Information Bureau, even the time of binding international conferences is over. But the world communist movement lives on.

All parties are completely and irreversibly independent. We declared that as early as the 20th Congress. True, the old habits were not discarded at once. But today this has become an unalterable reality.

In this sense, too, the 27th Congress of the CPSU was a final and irrevocable turning point. I think this has been actually proved by our relations with fraternal parties in the course of perestroika.

The world communist movement is at a turning point, just as is world progress itself and its motive forces.

The communist parties are looking for their new place in the context of the profound changes unfolding as we are about to enter a new century. Their international movement is undergoing a renewal, united by respect for the similarly renewed principles of confidence, equality and sincere solidarity.

The movement is open to dialogue, cooperation, interaction and alliance with any other revolutionary, democratic and progressive forces.

The heights reached enable us to have a clearer view of many things. Life has corrected our notions of the laws and rates of transition to socialism, our understanding of the role of socialism on the world scale.

It would never occur to us to claim that all the progressive changes in the world are due to socialism alone.

However, the way the problems of vital importance to humankind have been posed, the way solutions to them are being sought show that there is an inseparable link between world progress and socialism as an international force.

This link is brought into particularly sharp focus by the effort to avert nuclear catastrophe and by such a balance of world forces which enables various peoples to more successfully uphold the socio-political choice they have made.

The accumulated experience has ensured a better possibility of building relations between socialist countries on the following universally recognised principles:

— Unconditional and full equality;

— The ruling party's responsibility for the state of affairs in the country; its patriotic service to the people;

— Concern for the common cause of socialism;

— Respect for on another; a serious attitude to what has been achieved and tested by one's friends; voluntary and diverse cooperation;

— A strict observance of the principles of peaceful coexistence by all. This is what the practice of socialist internationalism rests on.

Today the socialist world appears before us in all its national and social variety. This is good and useful. We have satisfied ourselves that unity does not mean identity and uniformity. We have also become convinced of there being no "model" of socialism to be emulated by everyone.

The totality and quality of actual successes scored in restructuring society for the sake of the working people is the criterion of socialism's development at each stage and in each country.

We are aware of the damage that can be done to relations between socialist countries by a weakening of internationalist principles, by a departure from the principle of mutual benefit and mutual assistance, by a neglect of the common interests of socialism on the international scene.

We are gratified to state that of late our relations with all socialist states have become more dynamic and are being perfected. And cooperation in the framework of the Warsaw Treaty and CMEA certainly has become more fruitful and workmanlike, which incidentally does not set their member-countries in any essential way apart from other socialist countries.

The 27th Congress clearly defined the CPSU's position—in politics and all other areas of interaction with every socialist country, ensuring the combination of mutual interests with the interests of socialism as a whole is of decisive importance.

The strengthening of friendship and utmost development of cooperation with a socialist countries is the top-priority goal of the Soviet Union's foreign policy.

ABOUT THE AUTHOR

Dr. Allen Lynch is Deputy Director of Studies at the Institute for East-West Security Studies and an Adjunct Professor in the Department of Politics at New York University. His book on *The Soviet Study of International Relations* (Cambridge University Press, 1987) won the Marshall D. Shulman Prize of the American Association for the Advancement of Slavic Studies for the most outstanding book on Soviet foreign policy published in 1987. Dr. Lynch has published articles on Soviet foreign policy and international security issues in *Foreign Policy, Bulletin of the Atomic Scientists* and *Arms Control Today* and is the author of IEWSS Occasional Papers on U.S.-Soviet confidence-building measures and the nuclear winter theory.